CU00779604

The XXL Mediterranean Diet Cookbook

A Recipe Book with Affordable,
Delicious & Super-Amazing Dishes for Everyday
Enjoyment | incl. Breakfast, Dinner,
Desserts & More | Meal Plan for Beginners

Adam D. Gardner

Copyright © [2023] [Adam D. Gardner]

All rights reserved

The author of this book owns the exclusive right to its content.
Any commercial usage or reproduction requires the clear consent of the author.

ISBN - 9798853596368

Table of Contents

EXCLUSIVE BONUS

40 Weight Loss Recipes

&

14 Days Meal Plan

Scan the QR-Code and receive
the FREE download:

Introduction

Your Journey into the Mediterranean Lifestyle

Welcome to the vivacious and wholesome world of the Mediterranean diet, a lifestyle celebrated for its abundance of vibrant flavours and its undeniable health benefits. This culinary journey will introduce you to the glorious cuisine of the Mediterranean region, where simple ingredients are transformed into mouthwatering dishes that will take your taste buds on a sensational adventure. Get ready to embrace a way of eating that not only nourishes your body but also brings joy and pleasure to your everyday meals. In this book, we will explore the essence of the Mediterranean diet, which is not just a fleeting trend, but a time-honored tradition passed down through generations. Originating from the countries that border the Mediterranean Sea, this way of eating encompasses a wide variety of fresh fruits and vegetables, whole grains, legumes, nuts, seeds, olive oil, and lean proteins. With its emphasis on wholesome and minimally processed foods, this diet has been proven to promote heart health, reduce the risk of chronic diseases, and support overall well-being.

One of the key aspects of the Mediterranean diet is its simplicity. Rather than relying on complicated cooking techniques or heavy sauces, Mediterranean dishes celebrate the natural flavours of the ingredients. By using herbs, spices, and olive oil as the foundation of their culinary creations, Mediterranean cooks demonstrate that deliciousness can be achieved with just a handful of simple, affordable, and accessible ingredients. This means that you don't need to be an expert chef or have access to exotic ingredients to enjoy the wonderful flavours of the Mediterranean. Furthermore, the Mediterranean diet is a true celebration of the joy of eating together. In Mediterranean cultures, meals are often shared with family and friends, with food acting as a vehicle for connection and community. So, not only will you discover delicious recipes in this book, but you will also find inspiration to gather your loved ones around the table, creating memorable moments with every bite.

Whether you are looking to improve your health, adopt a more sustainable approach to eating, or simply broaden your culinary horizons, this book is your essential guide to embracing the Mediterranean lifestyle. Each recipe has been carefully crafted to offer a fusion of flavours that will transport you straight to the sun-kissed shores of the Mediterranean. From succulent seafood to hearty vegetarian dishes, from crisp salads to comforting stews, this collection has something for everyone. Moreover, the Mediterranean diet is not just about what you eat; it's also about how you approach food and your overall lifestyle. It encourages you to be mindful of your choices, to savour your meals, and to find balance in your day-to-day routine. Incorporating physical activity, such as walking or swimming, is also an essential part of the Mediterranean lifestyle, promoting overall health and well-being.

So, are you ready to embark on a culinary adventure like no other? Get ready to delight in the vibrant flavours of the Mediterranean, nourish your body with wholesome ingredients, and discover the true pleasure of eating well. With this book as your guide, you will become a master of Mediterranean cooking, and your kitchen will become a gateway to a world of delightful and nutritious dishes. Get ready to fall in love with the Mediterranean lifestyle, one delicious recipe at a time.

Essentials of the Mediterranean Diet

The Mediterranean diet has gained immense popularity over the years, and for good reason. It is not just a diet but a way of life that emphasizes fresh, whole foods, and a balanced approach to eating. Originating in the Mediterranean region, this diet has been associated with numerous health benefits and is considered one of the healthiest diets in the world. At its core, the Mediterranean diet is rich in fresh fruits and vegetables, whole grains, legumes, nuts, and seeds. This abundance of plant-based foods provides a wide array of vitamins, minerals, and antioxidants that help protect against chronic diseases such as heart disease, diabetes, and certain types of cancer. It is also low in processed foods, added sugars, and unhealthy fats, making it an excellent choice for weight management.

One of the essential components of the Mediterranean diet is olive oil. Traditional Mediterranean cuisine relies heavily on olive oil as the primary source of fat. Olive oil is rich in monounsaturated fats, which are known to promote heart health by reducing bad cholesterol levels and increasing good cholesterol levels. It also contains powerful antioxidants that help fight inflammation and oxidative stress in the body.

Another staple of the Mediterranean diet is fish and seafood. These sources of lean protein are consumed regularly and provide essential nutrients such as omega-3 fatty acids, which are known for their anti-inflammatory properties. Omega-3 fatty acids have been linked to a reduced risk of cardiovascular disease and improved brain health. In addition to fish, the Mediterranean diet includes moderate amounts of poultry, eggs, and dairy products, primarily in the form of yogurt and cheese. These animal products are consumed in smaller portions compared to plant-based foods, ensuring a balanced and wholesome eating pattern.

Interestingly, the Mediterranean diet also embraces red wine in moderation. Red wine, when consumed in moderation, has been associated with certain health benefits, mainly due to its high content of antioxidants such as resveratrol. However, it is important to note that excessive alcohol consumption can have detrimental effects on health, so moderation is key. The Mediterranean diet not only focuses on what foods to eat but also how they are prepared and enjoyed. This dietary pattern encourages cooking at home using fresh ingredients and limiting processed and fast foods. Herbs and spices are used to enhance the flavour of dishes, reducing the need for excessive salt and added sugars. Meals are often enjoyed with family and friends, promoting a sense of community and mindful eating.

Physical activity is another essential aspect of the Mediterranean lifestyle. Regular exercise, whether it be walking, swimming, or playing a sport, is encouraged to maintain overall health and wellbeing. This combination of a wholesome diet and an active lifestyle contributes to the long-term success and sustainability of the Mediterranean diet. The Mediterranean diet is not a strict set of rules but rather a flexible and adaptable approach to eating. It can be customized based on personal preferences and dietary needs. Whether you are vegetarian, vegan, or have dietary restrictions, there are plenty of options within the Mediterranean diet to suit your lifestyle.

In conclusion, the Mediterranean diet encompasses the consumption of fresh, whole foods, with a focus on plant-based ingredients, olive oil, fish, and moderate amounts of other animal products. It promotes a wholesome eating pattern, encourages physical activity, and embraces the social aspect of enjoying meals with loved ones. By adopting the Mediterranean diet, you can enjoy affordable, healthy, and super-amazing dishes for everyday enjoyment while reaping the many health benefits it has to offer.

What to Include in Your Mediterranean Diet

The Mediterranean diet is known for its health benefits and delicious and diverse dishes. It is a culinary approach that is inspired by the traditional eating habits of Mediterranean countries, such as Greece, Italy, and Spain. Following a Mediterranean diet can help you maintain a healthy weight, reduce the risk of chronic diseases, and improve overall well-being. In this article, we will explore some key components that you should include in your Mediterranean diet to fully enjoy its benefits.

1. **Fresh Fruits and Vegetables:** Incorporate a variety of fruits and vegetables into your meals. Opt for seasonal produce whenever possible, as it tends to be more flavourful and nutrient rich. Make colourful salads, roast vegetables as a side dish, or blend them into a smoothie for a refreshing and nutritious treat.

2. **Whole Grains:** Replace refined grains with whole grains such as whole wheat, brown rice, quinoa, and oats. Whole grains are a good source of fiber, which aids in digestion and helps you feel full for longer. Try whole grain pasta or bread, or experiment with ancient grains like bulgur or farro.

3. **Legumes:** Beans, lentils, and chickpeas are staple ingredients in the Mediterranean diet. They are rich in protein, fiber, and various minerals. Add them to soups, stews, or salads for a satisfying and nutritious meal. Hummus, made from chickpeas, is also a delicious and healthy dip or spread.

4. **Healthy Fats:** The Mediterranean diet emphasizes consuming healthy fats, such as those found in olive oil, nuts, and seeds. Olive oil is a key component of Mediterranean cooking and can be used for sautéing vegetables, drizzling over salads, or as a dip for bread. Nuts and seeds make for great snacks and can be sprinkled on top of yogurt or added to granola for an extra crunch.

5. **Fish and Seafood:** Fish and seafood play a significant role in the Mediterranean diet. They are excellent sources of omega-3 fatty acids, which are beneficial for heart health. Incorporate fish like salmon, sardines, or mackerel into your meals at least twice a week. If you are a vegetarian, you can explore plant-based sources of omega-3s like flaxseeds or chia seeds.

6. **Lean Proteins:** While the Mediterranean diet is not necessarily vegetarian, it promotes lean sources of protein like poultry, eggs, and dairy products. Opt for lean cuts of meat and include eggs and low-fat dairy products like Greek yogurt and feta cheese in your diet.

7. **Herbs and Spices:** The Mediterranean diet relies heavily on herbs and spices to add flavour to dishes, reducing the need for excessive salt or unhealthy additives. Experiment with aromatic herbs like basil, oregano, rosemary, and thyme to infuse your meals with Mediterranean flavours.

8. **Red Wine (in moderation):** Moderate consumption of red wine is a common practice in Mediterranean countries. If you drink alcohol, enjoying a glass of red wine with your meals can be part of a Mediterranean lifestyle. However, moderation is key, and excessive alcohol consumption can have detrimental health effects.

By incorporating these key components into your diet, you can enjoy a wide variety of tasty and nutritious meals while reaping the numerous benefits of the Mediterranean diet. Remember to focus on whole, unprocessed foods, and to savour mealtimes with family and friends. Embrace the Mediterranean way of eating, and you will discover a world of flavours that will nourish both your body and soul.

Foods to Sidestep in the Mediterranean Diet

The Mediterranean diet is renowned for its health benefits, promoting heart health, reducing the risk of chronic diseases, and aiding in weight management. This diet focuses on fresh, whole foods that are abundant in the Mediterranean region, such as fruits, vegetables, legumes, whole grains, olive oil, and fish. While it encourages a wide variety of nutrient-dense foods, there are a few foods that are best to be avoided or consumed in moderation to ensure optimal health benefits.

Processed meats, such as sausages, bacon, and deli meats, are high in unhealthy fats, sodium, and added preservatives, making them a poor choice for the Mediterranean diet. These meats are often linked to an increased risk of heart disease and certain cancers. Instead, opt for lean sources of protein like poultry, fish, legumes, and plant-based alternatives.

Fried foods, a staple in many Western diets, are also best avoided within the Mediterranean diet. These foods are often high in unhealthy fats and calories, contributing to weight gain and an increased risk of heart disease. Instead, try grilling, baking, or steaming foods to retain their nutritional value while reducing unnecessary added fats.

Refined grains, such as white bread, pasta, and rice, have minimal nutritional value compared to their whole grain counterparts. The refining process removes the bran and germ, stripping away essential fiber, vitamins, and minerals. Instead, choose whole grains like quinoa, whole wheat bread, and brown rice that contain more fiber and nutrients to support a healthy digestive system and steady blood sugar levels.

Sugary beverages, including soda, fruit juices, and energy drinks, are high in added sugars and empty calories. These drinks can contribute to weight gain, obesity, and an increased risk of chronic diseases such as type 2 diabetes and heart disease. Opt for water, herbal tea, or infusions of fruits and herbs to stay hydrated and refresh your palate without added sugars. Sweets and desserts are often indulged in moderation within the Mediterranean diet. However, it is important to limit the consumption of pastries, cakes, cookies, and ice cream due to their high sugar and unhealthy fat content. Instead, satisfy your sweet tooth with fresh fruits, Greek yogurt with honey, or a homemade fruit sorbet using natural ingredients.

While red meat, such as beef and pork, is not entirely excluded from the Mediterranean diet, it is recommended to consume it in moderation. High consumption of red meat has been linked to an increased risk of heart disease and certain cancers. To incorporate protein into your diet, focus on lean sources like fish, poultry, legumes, and tofu. Lastly, it is important to moderate alcohol consumption within the Mediterranean diet. While moderate intake of red wine has been associated with some health benefits, excessive alcohol consumption can have negative effects on overall health. It is crucial to drink in moderation and be mindful of the potential risks associated with excessive alcohol consumption.

By avoiding or limiting these foods in your Mediterranean diet, you can enhance the health benefits and fully embrace the nutritious and delicious foods that this eating pattern has to offer.

Remember, the Mediterranean diet is not a strict set of rules but rather a flexible approach to eating that emphasizes the enjoyment of fresh, whole foods in moderation.

Embarking on the Mediterranean Diet: A Step-by-step Guide

The Mediterranean Diet has gained immense popularity in recent years for its health benefits and delicious, wholesome dishes. Originating from the Mediterranean region, this diet focuses on consuming fresh fruits and vegetables, whole grains, lean proteins, and healthy fats. It is not just a diet but a lifestyle that emphasizes moderation, enjoyment, and the celebration of food.

If you are considering adopting the Mediterranean Diet, here is a step-by-step guide to help you get started on this incredible journey.

Step 1: Educate Yourself

Before diving into any new diet, it is essential to educate yourself about its principles, benefits, and food choices. Learn about the Mediterranean region, its traditional cuisine, and the philosophy behind this lifestyle. Understand the health benefits associated with this diet, such as reduced risk of heart disease, improved brain health, and overall well-being. By understanding the why, you will be motivated to make lasting changes in your eating habits.

Step 2: Stock Your Kitchen

To follow the Mediterranean Diet, make sure your kitchen is stocked with key ingredients. Load up on fresh fruits and vegetables, whole grains like quinoa and brown rice, legumes such as chickpeas and lentils, and a variety of nuts and seeds. In addition, include seafood like salmon and sardines, lean meats, and poultry in moderation. Don't forget to have extra virgin olive oil, herbs, and spices to add flavour to your dishes.

Step 3: Plan Your Meals

Meal planning is crucial to successful adherence to any diet. Start by incorporating Mediterranean-inspired dishes into your weekly menu. Experiment with colourful salads, vegetable-packed soups, whole grain pastas, and fish-based meals. Consider using traditional Mediterranean ingredients like feta cheese, olives, and garlic to add a burst of flavour to your meals. Planning your meals in advance will help you stay on track and make healthier choices.

Step 4: Emphasize Fruits and Vegetables

One of the core principles of the Mediterranean Diet is the abundant consumption of fruits and vegetables. Aim to fill half of your plate with various types of fruits and vegetables at each meal. Experiment with seasonal produce and explore different cooking methods such as roasting, grilling, or steaming. Not only will this add a variety of flavours to your meals, but it will also provide your body with essential vitamins, minerals, and fiber.

Step 5: Incorporate Healthy Fats and Whole Grains

The Mediterranean Diet encourages the consumption of healthy fats and whole grains. Replace unhealthy fats like butter or margarine with olive oil, which is rich in antioxidants and monounsaturated fats. Include whole grains such as oatmeal, whole wheat bread, and whole grain pasta to boost your fiber intake. These food choices will help you feel satiated and provide sustained energy throughout the day.

Step 6: Enjoy Lean Proteins and Seafood

Incorporate lean proteins into your meals, such as chicken breast, turkey, and tofu. Seafood, such as salmon, sardines, and mackerel, are rich in omega-3 fatty acids, which have numerous health benefits. Aim to consume fish at least twice a week, combining it with fresh vegetables for a balanced and nutritious meal.

Step 7: Practice Portion Control and Mindful Eating

The Mediterranean Diet emphasizes portion control and mindful eating. Listen to your body's hunger and fullness cues and avoid overeating. Slow down your eating pace, savour the flavours, and enjoy your meals without distractions. Eating mindfully will not only help you control your portion sizes but also enhance your overall dining experience.

Step 8: Stay Hydrated and Be Active

To maintain a healthy lifestyle, staying hydrated and being physically active are crucial. Drink plenty of water throughout the day and limit sugary beverages. Incorporate regular physical activity into your routine, whether it's going for a walk, practicing yoga, or engaging in a sport you enjoy. Stay active to support your overall health and complement the benefits of the Mediterranean Diet.

By following these steps, you can successfully embark on the Mediterranean Diet and enjoy a wide array of delicious, healthy, and super-amazing dishes every day. Embrace this lifestyle, savour the flavours, and reap the many benefits that come from nourishing your body with wholesome Mediterranean cuisine.

Pave the Way to a Healthier Future

The Mediterranean diet has long been hailed as a healthy and delicious way of eating. With its emphasis on fresh fruits and vegetables, whole grains, lean proteins, and heart-healthy fats, it is no wonder that people who follow this lifestyle tend to have lower rates of heart disease, obesity, and certain types of cancer. In fact, research has consistently shown that the Mediterranean diet is one of the best ways to improve overall health and wellbeing.

One of the key components of the Mediterranean diet is the abundant use of fresh, seasonal ingredients. This means that meals are packed with vitamins, minerals, and antioxidants that support good health. Fruits and vegetables are staples, making up a large portion of every meal. These nutrient-dense foods are low in calories and high in fiber, making them perfect for weight management and promoting digestive health. Another important aspect of the Mediterranean diet is the inclusion of whole grains. Unlike their refined counterparts, whole grains retain all parts of the grain, including the bran, germ, and endosperm. This means that they are high in fiber, B vitamins, and essential minerals. Whole grains have been linked to a reduced risk of heart disease, type 2 diabetes, and certain types of cancer. Plus, they keep you feeling fuller for longer, making it easier to maintain a healthy weight.

The Mediterranean diet also encourages the consumption of lean proteins, such as fish, poultry, legumes, and nuts. These proteins are rich in essential amino acids and omega-3 fatty acids, which are known to have numerous health benefits. Omega-3 fatty acids, in particular, have been shown to reduce inflammation in the body, improve brain health, and lower the risk of chronic diseases like heart disease and Alzheimer's. One of the most unique features of the Mediterranean diet is its use of heart-healthy fats. Instead of relying on saturated and trans fats, which are known to raise cholesterol levels and increase the risk of heart disease, the Mediterranean diet favors healthier fats like olive oil, avocados, and nuts. These fats not only add delicious flavour to meals but also provide important nutrients like vitamin E and monounsaturated fats, which have been shown to reduce the risk of heart disease.

In addition to its many health benefits, the Mediterranean diet is also incredibly versatile and delicious. It embraces the flavours and cuisines of countries like Greece, Italy, Spain, and Turkey, offering a wide variety of dishes to suit every taste. From fresh Greek salads and flavourful Italian pastas to Moroccan-spiced grilled fish and Spanish tapas, the Mediterranean diet is a culinary adventure that will never leave you bored or unsatisfied. Implementing the Mediterranean diet into your everyday life is easier than you might think. By focusing on whole, unprocessed foods and making simple swaps in your cooking techniques and ingredient choices, you can start enjoying the benefits right away. And with the abundance of fresh produce and ingredients available in the UK, it has never been more accessible or affordable to follow this healthy and super-amazing way of eating.

So, why not pave the way to a healthier future by embracing the Mediterranean diet? Not only will you be nourishing your body with the nutrients it needs to thrive, but you will also be enjoying delicious meals that are easy to prepare and enjoy.

Chapter 1: Wholesome Breakfasts (20 Recipes)

Mediterranean Sunrise Shakshuka

Servings: 2 | Preparation time: 15 minutes

Ingredients

- 2 tablespoons olive oil
- 1 red bell pepper, thinly sliced
- 1 yellow bell pepper, thinly sliced
- 1 small red onion, thinly sliced
- 2 cloves garlic, minced
- 1 teaspoon ground cumin
- 1 teaspoon paprika
- 1/2 teaspoon chili flakes (optional, for spice lovers)
- 400g can chopped tomatoes
- 4 large free-range eggs
- Salt and pepper, to taste
- Fresh parsley, chopped (for garnish)
- Crusty bread, to serve

Nutrition facts per 100g:

Calories: 115
Total Fat: 7g
Saturated Fat: 1g
Cholesterol: 107mg
Sodium: 148mg
Total Carbohydrate: 8g
Dietary Fiber: 2g
Sugars: 4g
Protein: 5g

Preparation:

1. Heat the olive oil in a large frying pan over medium heat. Add the bell peppers and onion and cook for 5 minutes until softened.
2. Add the minced garlic, cumin, paprika, and chili flakes (if using) to the pan. Stir well to coat the vegetables evenly with the spices.
3. Pour in the chopped tomatoes and season with salt and pepper. Simmer the mixture for about 10 minutes until the sauce has thickened.
4. Make small wells in the sauce and crack an egg into each well. Cover the pan and let the eggs cook for about 5 minutes or until the whites are set but the yolks are still runny.
5. Remove the pan from heat and sprinkle freshly chopped parsley over the shakshuka.
6. Serve the Mediterranean Sunrise Shakshuka in shallow bowls with crusty bread on the side for dipping.

Greek-Style Yoghurt Parfait

Servings: 2 | Preparation time: 10-15 minutes

Ingredients

- 200g Greek-style yoghurt
- 100g granola
- 2 tablespoons honey
- 1 medium-sized banana, sliced.
- 100g mixed berries (e.g., blueberries, raspberries, strawberries)
- 20g unsalted nuts, chopped (e.g., almonds, walnuts)

Nutrition facts per 100g:

Energy: 142 calories
Fat: 6.5g
Saturated Fat: 1.9g
Carbohydrates: 15.3g
Sugars: 6.5g
Fiber: 1.6g
Protein: 4.7g

Preparation:

1. In two glasses or bowls, start layering your wholesome breakfast. Begin with a spoonful of Greek-style yoghurt at the bottom of each glass.
2. Sprinkle a layer of granola on top of the yoghurt in each glass.
3. Drizzle a tablespoon of honey over the granola in each glass.
4. Add a layer of sliced banana to each glass.
5. Top the bananas with a handful of mixed berries in each glass.
6. Repeat the layers - add Greek-style yoghurt, granola, honey, banana slices, and mixed berries to each glass.
7. Finish off each glass with a sprinkle of chopped unsalted nuts on top.
8. Serve the Greek-Style Yoghurt Parfait immediately and enjoy a wholesome breakfast to start your day!

Spanish Tortilla Bites

Servings: 4 | Preparation time: 25-30 minutes

Ingredients

- 4 medium potatoes (approx. 600g), peeled and thinly sliced
- 1 small onion, finely chopped
- 6 large eggs
- 150ml extra-virgin olive oil
- Salt and pepper, to taste

Nutrition facts per 100g:

Calories: 241
Total Fat: 16.7g
Saturated Fat: 3.1g
Trans Fat: 0g
Total Carbohydrate: 17.8g
Dietary Fiber: 2.1g
Sugars: 1.6g
Protein: 6.3g

Preparation:

1. Heat half of the olive oil in a large frying pan over medium heat. Add the sliced potatoes and cook for about 10 minutes until tender, stirring occasionally.
2. In a separate frying pan, heat the remaining olive oil. Add the chopped onion and cook until it turns translucent and slightly golden.
3. In a large mixing bowl, beat the eggs and season with salt and pepper. Add the cooked potatoes and onion and stir everything together gently to combine.
4. Preheat the oven to 180°C (350°F).
5. Heat a medium-sized non-stick frying pan over medium heat. Add a small amount of oil if necessary.
6. Pour the potato and egg mixture into the pan and cook for 3-4 minutes until the edges start to set.
7. Transfer the pan to the preheated oven and bake for 12-15 minutes, or until the tortilla is set in the center.
8. Remove the pan from the oven and let it cool for a few minutes.
9. Cut the tortilla into small bite-sized squares or triangles and serve warm or at room temperature.

Olive and Feta Scramble

Servings: 2 | Preparation time: 10 minutes

Ingredients

- 4 large eggs
- 50g feta cheese, crumbled
- 6-8 cherry tomatoes, halved
- 8-10 black olives, sliced
- 1 tablespoon fresh parsley, finely chopped
- 1 tablespoon olive oil
- Salt and pepper to taste

Nutrition facts per 100g:

Calories: 197
Protein: 12.9g
Carbohydrates: 3.2g
Fat: 14.8g
Saturated fat: 4.7g
Cholesterol: 346mg
Fiber: 0.9g

Preparation:

1. Crack the eggs into a bowl and lightly whisk them with a fork.
2. Heat the olive oil in a non-stick frying pan over medium heat.
3. Add the cherry tomatoes to the pan and cook for 2-3 minutes until they begin to soften.
4. Stir in the black olives and cook for another minute.
5. Pour the whisked eggs into the pan and let them cook undisturbed for a few seconds until they start to set around the edges.
6. Use a spatula to gently scramble the eggs, breaking them up into smaller pieces.
7. Sprinkle the feta cheese over the eggs and continue cooking for 1-2 minutes, until the eggs are fully cooked, and the cheese starts to melt.
8. Season with salt and pepper to taste.
9. Remove the pan from heat and sprinkle the scrambled eggs with fresh parsley.
10. Divide the scrambled eggs onto plates and serve.

Seville Citrus Granola

Servings: 6 | Preparation time: 25 minutes

Ingredients

- 200g rolled oats
- 50g almonds, roughly chopped
- 50g pumpkin seeds
- 50g dried cranberries
- 50g dried apricots, chopped
- 2 tablespoons honey
- Zest of 1 orange
- Zest of 1 lemon
- Juice of 1 orange
- 1 tablespoon olive oil

Nutrition facts per 100g:

Calories: 414
Total Fat: 18.5g
Saturated Fat: 2.1g
Cholesterol: 0mg
Sodium: 4mg
Total Carbohydrate: 53.7g
Dietary Fiber: 7.9g
Sugars: 22.3g
Protein: 10.2g

Preparation:

1. Preheat the oven to 180°C and line a baking tray with parchment paper.
2. In a large bowl, combine the rolled oats, almonds, pumpkin seeds, dried cranberries, and dried apricots.
3. In a small saucepan, heat the honey, orange zest, lemon zest, orange juice, and olive oil over low heat. Stir until the mixture is well combined and slightly warmed.
4. Pour the honey mixture over the dry ingredients and mix well until everything is evenly coated.
5. Spread the granola mixture evenly onto the prepared baking tray.
6. Bake in the preheated oven for 20-25 minutes, or until the granola turns golden brown, stirring occasionally to prevent burning.
7. Allow the granola to cool completely on the baking tray. It will become crisp as it cools.
8. Once cooled, transfer the Seville Citrus Granola to an airtight container or glass jar and store in a cool, dry place.
9. Serve the granola with your choice of milk, yogurt, or fresh fruit for a wholesome Mediterranean-style breakfast.

Italian-style Bruschetta Toast

Servings: 2 | Preparation time: 10 minutes

Ingredients

- 4 slices of whole grain bread (200g)
- 2 large ripe tomatoes, diced (300g)
- 1 small red onion, finely chopped (60g)
- 2 cloves of garlic, minced
- 2 tbsp extra virgin olive oil (30ml)
- 1 tbsp balsamic vinegar (15ml)
- 8 fresh basil leaves, chopped
- Salt and pepper to taste

Nutrition facts per 100g:

Calories: 173
Total Fat: 6.5g
Saturated Fat: 1g
Trans Fat: 0g
Cholesterol: 0mg
Sodium: 186mg
Total Carbohydrate: 24.7g
Dietary Fiber: 4.4g
Sugars: 5.5g
Protein: 5.2g

Preparation:

1. Preheat the grill on medium-high heat.
2. In a bowl, combine the diced tomatoes, chopped red onion, minced garlic, olive oil, balsamic vinegar, and chopped basil leaves. Mix well.
3. Season the tomato mixture with salt and pepper according to your taste.
4. Toast the slices of whole grain bread under the grill until lightly golden on both sides.
5. Remove the toasts from the grill and let them cool slightly.
6. Divide the tomato mixture evenly onto the toasted bread slices.
7. Drizzle any remaining dressing from the bowl over the bruschetta toasts.
8. Sprinkle some additional chopped basil leaves on top for garnish if desired.
9. Serve the Italian-style bruschetta toasts immediately and enjoy!

Honeyed Halloumi & Tomato Skewers

Servings: 4 | Preparation time: 25 Minutes

Ingredients

- 225g halloumi cheese, cut into bite-sized cubes
- 200g cherry tomatoes
- 2 tablespoons olive oil
- 2 tablespoons honey
- 1 tablespoon balsamic vinegar
- 2 tablespoons fresh basil leaves, chopped
- Salt and pepper, to taste

Nutrition facts per 100g:

Calories: 300
Total Fat: 21g
Saturated Fat: 12g
Cholesterol: 50mg
Sodium: 500mg
Total Carbohydrate: 14g
Sugars: 9g
Protein: 15g

Preparation:

1. Preheat the grill or barbecue to medium-high heat.
2. Soak wooden skewers in water for about 10 minutes to prevent them from burning.
3. Thread the halloumi cubes and cherry tomatoes onto the skewers, alternating between the two.
4. In a small bowl, whisk together the olive oil, honey, balsamic vinegar, and chopped basil leaves.
5. Season the skewers with salt and pepper, then brush them generously with the honey-balsamic mixture.
6. Grill or barbecue the skewers for about 6-8 minutes, turning them occasionally, until the halloumi is golden brown, and the tomatoes are slightly blistered.
7. Transfer the skewers to a serving platter and drizzle with any remaining honey-balsamic mixture.
8. Serve the honeyed halloumi and tomato skewers as a wholesome breakfast option or as a vibrant appetizer.

Savoury Breakfast Quinoa with Olives

Servings: 2 | Preparation time: 25 minutes

Ingredients

- 150g quinoa
- 300ml vegetable or chicken broth
- 1 tablespoon olive oil
- 1 small onion, finely chopped
- 2 cloves of garlic, minced
- 10 Kalamata olives, pitted and chopped
- 1 red bell pepper, diced
- 2 sun-dried tomatoes, thinly sliced
- 1 teaspoon dried oregano
- Salt and black pepper to taste
- Handful of fresh parsley, chopped, for garnish

Nutrition facts per 100g:

Calories: 160
Total Fat: 5g
Saturated Fat: 0.6g
Total Carbohydrate: 24g
Dietary Fiber: 2.5g
Total Sugars: 1g
Protein: 4g

Preparation:

1. Rinse the quinoa under cold water and drain.
2. In a saucepan, bring the vegetable or chicken broth to a boil. Add the quinoa, reduce the heat to low, cover, and simmer for about 15 minutes until the liquid is absorbed and the quinoa is tender.
3. In the meantime, heat the olive oil in a frying pan over medium heat. Add the onion and garlic, and sauté until they become translucent.
4. Stir in the olives, red bell pepper, sun-dried tomatoes, dried oregano, salt, and black pepper. Cook for an additional 3-4 minutes until the vegetables are tender.
5. Once the quinoa is cooked, fluff it with a fork and transfer it to the frying pan with the sautéed vegetables. Mix everything together until well combined.
6. Cook for an additional 2-3 minutes, stirring occasionally. Adjust the seasoning if needed.
7. Divide the Savoury Breakfast Quinoa with Olives into bowls and garnish with freshly chopped parsley.
8. Serve hot and enjoy this wholesome and flavourful Mediterranean breakfast!

Mediterranean Breakfast Salad

Servings: 2 | Preparation time: 10 minutes

Ingredients

- 200g cherry tomatoes, halved
- 100g cucumber, diced
- 50g red onion, thinly sliced
- 50g Kalamata olives, pitted and halved
- 2 tbsp extra virgin olive oil
- 1 tbsp fresh lemon juice
- 1/2 tsp dried oregano
- Salt and pepper, to taste
- 100g feta cheese, crumbled
- 2 large eggs
- Fresh parsley, chopped (for garnish)

Nutrition facts per 100g:

Calories: 125
Total Fat: 10.5g
Saturated Fat: 4.3g
Total Carbohydrate: 4.1g
Dietary Fiber: 0.7g
Sugars: 1.7g
Protein: 4.6g

Preparation:

1. In a large bowl, combine the cherry tomatoes, cucumber, red onion, and Kalamata olives.
2. In a small bowl, whisk together the olive oil, lemon juice, dried oregano, salt, and pepper. Pour the dressing over the vegetables and toss to coat evenly.
3. Divide the salad between two serving plates.
4. Sprinkle the crumbled feta cheese over the salads.
5. Fill a medium-sized saucepan with water and bring it to a gentle simmer over medium heat.
6. Crack the eggs into separate small bowls or ramekins. Carefully slide each egg into the simmering water and cook for about 3-4 minutes, or until the whites are set but the yolks are still runny.
7. Using a slotted spoon, carefully remove the poached eggs from the water and place one on top of each salad.
8. Garnish with freshly chopped parsley and serve immediately.

Greek Yogurt and Honey Pancakes

Servings: 4 servings | Preparation time: 20 Minutes

Ingredients

- 200g plain Greek yogurt
- 2 eggs
- 2 tablespoons honey
- 150g whole wheat flour
- 1 teaspoon baking powder
- 1/4 teaspoon salt
- 1 teaspoon vanilla extract
- Cooking oil, for greasing the pan
- Honey, to serve
- Fresh fruits, such as berries or sliced bananas, to serve

Nutrition facts per 100g:

Calories: 224
Total Fat: 4.4g
Saturated Fat: 1.7g
Total Carbohydrate: 37.3g
Dietary Fiber: 4.7g
Sugars: 11.6g
Protein: 9.8g

Preparation:

1. In a mixing bowl, whisk together the Greek yogurt, eggs, and honey until well combined.
2. In a separate bowl, combine the whole wheat flour, baking powder, and salt.
3. Gradually add the dry ingredients to the wet ingredients, stirring well after each addition. Mix until you have a smooth pancake batter.
4. Stir in the vanilla extract.
5. Heat a non-stick pan or griddle over medium heat and lightly grease with cooking oil.
6. Drop about 1/4 cup of batter onto the pan for each pancake. Cook until bubbles form on the surface, then flip and cook for an additional 2-3 minutes until golden brown.
7. Repeat the process with the remaining batter, adding more oil as needed.
8. Serve the pancakes warm, drizzled with honey, and topped with fresh fruits.

Hearty Lentil and Veggie Breakfast Bowl

Servings: 2 | Preparation time: 30-40 Minutes

Ingredients

- 100g dried green lentils
- 1 small red onion, diced
- 1 red bell pepper, diced
- 1 zucchini, diced
- 2 garlic cloves, minced
- 1 tablespoon olive oil
- 1 teaspoon dried oregano
- 1/2 teaspoon paprika
- Salt and pepper to taste
- 2 large eggs
- Fresh herbs for garnish (such as parsley or chives)

Nutrition facts per 100g:

Calories: 112
Protein: 5g
Fat: 4g
Carbohydrates: 15 g
Sugar: 2g

Preparation:

1. Rinse the lentils under cold water, then place them in a saucepan with 250ml of water. Bring to a boil, then reduce the heat and simmer for 15-20 minutes until the lentils are tender. Drain any excess water and set aside.
2. In a large frying pan, heat the olive oil over medium heat. Add the diced red onion and cook for 3-4 minutes until softened.
3. Add the diced red bell pepper, zucchini, and minced garlic to the pan. Cook for another 5 minutes until the vegetables are slightly softened.
4. Stir in the cooked lentils, dried oregano, and paprika. Season with salt and pepper to taste. Continue cooking for another 2-3 minutes until all the flavours are well combined.
5. In a separate non-stick frying pan, fry the eggs to your liking (e.g., sunny-side-up, poached, or scrambled).
6. Divide the lentil and veggie mixture between two bowls. Top each bowl with a fried egg and garnish with fresh herbs.
7. Serve the hearty lentil and veggie breakfast bowl immediately, while still warm.

Cretan Barley Rusks (Dakos)

Servings: 4 | Preparation time: 15 minutes

Ingredients

- 4 large barley rusks
- 4 medium tomatoes, diced
- 1 cucumber, peeled and diced
- 1 red onion, thinly sliced
- 100g feta cheese, crumbled
- 4 tablespoons extra-virgin olive oil
- 1 tablespoon dried oregano
- Salt and pepper to taste
- Fresh parsley or mint, chopped (for garnish)

Nutrition facts per 100g:

Calories: 138
Protein: 5.8g
Carbohydrates: 21g
Fat: 4.6g
Saturated Fat: 2g
Fiber: 2.6g
Sugar: 3.2g

Preparation:

1. Soak the barley rusks in water for a few seconds to soften them slightly, then drain.
2. Place the rusks on a flat surface and lightly sprinkle them with water to moisten.
3. In a bowl, combine the diced tomatoes, cucumber, and red onion.
4. Season the tomato mixture with salt, pepper, and dried oregano. Mix well.
5. Drizzle each rusk with a tablespoon of extra-virgin olive oil.
6. Top the rusks with the tomato mixture, dividing it evenly.
7. Sprinkle the crumbled feta cheese over the tomatoes.
8. Garnish with chopped parsley or mint.
9. Serve immediately and enjoy your wholesome Cretan barley rusks for breakfast!

Mediterranean Frittata with Zucchini and Feta

Servings: 4 | Preparation time: 20 minutes

Ingredients

- 6 large eggs
- 1 zucchini, thinly sliced
- 1 red bell pepper, thinly sliced
- 1 small red onion, thinly sliced
- 100g feta cheese, crumbled
- Handful of fresh basil leaves, torn
- 2 tablespoons olive oil
- Salt and pepper, to taste

Nutrition facts per 100g:

Calories: 156
Protein: 9g
Fat: 12g
Carbohydrates: 2g
Fiber: 0g
Sugar: 1g

Preparation:

1. Preheat your oven to 180°C (350°F).
2. Heat the olive oil in a large ovenproof skillet over medium heat. Add the sliced zucchini, bell pepper, and red onion, and sauté until softened, about 5 minutes. Remove from heat and set aside.
3. In a mixing bowl, whisk the eggs until well beaten. Season with salt and pepper to taste.
4. Pour the beaten eggs over the sautéed vegetables in the skillet. Sprinkle the crumbled feta cheese evenly on top.
5. Transfer the skillet to the preheated oven and bake for 15-20 minutes or until the frittata is set and slightly golden on top.
6. Remove from the oven and allow the frittata to cool for a few minutes.
7. Sprinkle torn basil leaves on top for added freshness and flavour.
8. Slice the frittata into wedges and serve warm as a satisfying breakfast or brunch option.

Egg & Spinach Pita Pocket

Servings: 2 | Preparation time: 15 minutes

Ingredients

- 4 large eggs
- 100g baby spinach leaves
- 1 small red onion, finely chopped
- 1 garlic clove, minced
- 1 tablespoon olive oil
- 2 wholemeal pita breads
- Salt to taste
- Black pepper to taste

Nutrition facts per 100g:

Calories: 141 kcal
Total Fat: 7.5g
Saturated Fat: 1.7g
Trans Fat: 0g
Total Carbohydrate: 12.9g
Dietary Fiber: 2.4g
Sugars: 1.8g
Protein: 7.8g

Preparation:

1. In a non-stick frying pan, heat the olive oil over medium heat. Add the chopped red onion and minced garlic, and cook until softened and slightly browned, about 3 minutes.
2. Add the baby spinach leaves to the pan and cook until wilted, stirring occasionally, for about 2 minutes. Season with salt and black pepper.
3. In a separate bowl, lightly beat the eggs and then pour them into the pan with the spinach mixture. Gently scramble the eggs until cooked through, about 3-4 minutes.
4. While the eggs are cooking, carefully cut the wholemeal pita breads in half to form pockets.
5. Once the eggs are cooked, divide the egg and spinach mixture evenly among the pita pockets. You can gently press down to compact them.
6. Serve the egg and spinach pita pockets warm and enjoy a wholesome and nutritious Mediterranean-inspired breakfast!

Sweet Greek Crepes with Honey & Walnuts

Servings: 4 | Preparation time: 20 Minutes

Ingredients

- 200g all-purpose flour
- 2 large eggs
- 300ml milk
- 2 tablespoons olive oil, plus extra for cooking
- Pinch of salt
- 100g walnuts, roughly chopped
- 4 tablespoons Greek honey
- Fresh berries, to serve (optional)
- Greek yogurt, to serve (optional)

Nutrition facts per 100g:

Calories: 314
Total Fat: 15g
Saturated Fat: 2g
Total Carbohydrate: 40g
Dietary Fiber: 2g
Sugars: 14g
Protein: 7g

Preparation:

1. In a large mixing bowl, combine the flour, eggs, milk, olive oil, and salt. Whisk vigorously until you have a smooth batter. Let it rest for 10 minutes.
2. Heat a non-stick frying pan over medium heat. Lightly grease the pan with a little olive oil.
3. Pour a ladleful of the batter into the pan, swirling it around to evenly coat the base. Cook for about 2 minutes, or until the edges start to turn golden.
4. Flip the crepe and cook for a further 1-2 minutes until lightly golden. Set aside on a warm plate and repeat the process with the remaining batter.
5. In a small dry pan, toast the walnuts over low heat for 2-3 minutes until fragrant. Remove from heat and set aside.
6. To serve, drizzle each crepe with a tablespoon of Greek honey and sprinkle with a handful of toasted walnuts. Add fresh berries if desired.
7. Fold the crepe in half, then in quarters or roll it up. Serve warm with a dollop of Greek yogurt on the side for extra creaminess.

Green Olive Tapenade on Wholegrain Toast

Servings: 4 | Preparation time: 20 minutes

Ingredients

- 200g pitted green olives
- 2 tablespoons capers, drained
- 2 cloves of garlic, minced
- 1 tablespoon lemon juice
- 1 tablespoon extra virgin olive oil
- 1 tablespoon fresh parsley, chopped
- 4 slices of wholegrain bread

Nutrition facts per 100g:

Calories: 160 kcal
Total Fat: 14g
Saturated Fat: 2g
Trans Fat: 0g
Total Carbohydrate: 8g
Dietary Fiber: 4g
Sugars: 0g
Protein: 2g

Preparation:

1. In a food processor, add the green olives, capers, minced garlic, lemon juice, and extra virgin olive oil.
2. Blend until you achieve a smooth and spreadable consistency.
3. Transfer the tapenade to a bowl and stir in the chopped parsley. Set aside.
4. Toast the wholegrain bread slices until they are golden brown and crispy.
5. Once toasted, spread a generous amount of the green olive tapenade on each slice of bread.
6. Serve the wholesome breakfast by pairing the toast with a side of fresh fruit or a cup of herbal tea.

Tomato and Basil Savoury Oatmeal

Servings: 2 | Preparation time: 15 Minutes

Ingredients

- 150g rolled oats
- 400ml water
- 200g cherry tomatoes, halved
- 1 small red onion, finely chopped
- 2 cloves of garlic, minced
- 2 tbsp fresh basil leaves, torn
- 2 tbsp balsamic vinegar
- 2 tbsp olive oil
- Salt and pepper, to taste

Nutrition facts per 100g:

Calories: 118 kcal
Protein: 3.3g
Fat: 4.6g
Carbohydrates: 16.7g
Fiber: 2.8g
Sugar: 3.2g

Preparation:

1. In a saucepan, combine the rolled oats and water. Bring to a boil over medium heat, then reduce the heat to low and simmer for about 5 minutes until the oats are cooked and thickened.
2. Meanwhile, in a frying pan, heat olive oil over medium heat. Add the red onion and garlic, and sauté for 2-3 minutes until softened.
3. Add the cherry tomatoes to the pan and cook for another 3-4 minutes until they soften and release their juices. Stir occasionally to prevent sticking.
4. Sprinkle the balsamic vinegar over the tomato mixture and cook for an additional 2 minutes to allow the flavours to meld. Season with salt and pepper to taste.
5. Stir in the torn basil leaves and remove the pan from heat.
6. Divide the cooked oats into two bowls. Spoon the tomato and basil mixture over the oats.
7. Serve the tomato and basil savoury oatmeal warm, and garnish with additional torn basil leaves if desired.

Roasted Pepper and Hummus Wrap

Servings: 2 | Preparation time: 20 minutes

Ingredients

- 2 large red bell peppers
- 4 tablespoons hummus
- 2 large whole wheat wraps
- 1 small cucumber, thinly sliced
- 1 medium tomato, thinly sliced
- Handful of fresh basil leaves
- Salt and pepper, to taste

Nutrition facts per 100g:

Calories: 95
Total Fat: 2.5g
Saturated Fat: 0.4g
Total Carbohydrate: 16g
Dietary Fiber: 4g
Sugars: 4g
Protein: 3.5g

Preparation:

1. Preheat the oven to 200°C (180°C fan) and line a baking tray with parchment paper.
2. Cut the bell peppers into quarters, remove the seeds, and place them skin-side up on the baking tray.
3. Roast the peppers in the preheated oven for about 20 minutes or until the skin starts to blister and turn black.
4. Remove from the oven and allow the peppers to cool for a few minutes. Once cooled, peel off the skin and discard.
5. Lay the wraps on a clean surface and spread 2 tablespoons of hummus onto each wrap.
6. Place the roasted peppers, cucumber slices, tomato slices, and fresh basil leaves on top of the hummus.
7. Season with salt and pepper to taste.
8. Roll each wrap tightly, tucking in the ends as you go.
9. Cut the wraps in half and serve immediately.

Avocado and Chickpea Toast

Servings: 2 | Preparation time: 10 minutes

Ingredients

- 2 slices of whole grain bread
- 1 ripe avocado
- 1 small garlic clove, minced
- 1/2 cup canned chickpeas, drained and rinsed
- 1 small tomato, diced
- 1/4 red onion, finely chopped
- 1/2 lemon, juiced
- 1 tablespoon extra virgin olive oil
- Salt and black pepper, to taste
- Fresh parsley, chopped (for garnish)

Nutrition facts per 100g:

Calories: 246
Fat: 12.7g
Saturated Fat: 1.8g
Carbohydrates: 31.5g
Fiber: 9.5g
Sugar: 2.5g
Protein: 6.7g

Preparation:

1. Toast the slices of bread until crunchy and golden brown.
2. Cut the avocado in half, remove the pit, and scoop out the flesh into a bowl.
3. Mash the avocado with a fork until smooth, and then add minced garlic and a squeeze of lemon juice. Mix well.
4. In a separate bowl, lightly mash the chickpeas with a fork, leaving some chunks for texture.
5. Add the chopped tomato and onion to the chickpeas, and drizzle with olive oil. Season with salt and pepper to taste.
6. Spread the avocado mixture generously onto each slice of toast.
7. Top the avocado with the chickpea mixture, spreading it evenly.
8. Garnish with freshly chopped parsley.
9. Serve your wholesome avocado and chickpea toast immediately and enjoy!

Fig and Ricotta Toast with Honey Drizzle

Servings: 2 | Preparation time: 10 minutes

Ingredients

- 4 slices of whole grain bread
- 150g ricotta cheese
- 4 ripe figs, thinly sliced
- 2 tbsp honey
- 2 tsp chopped fresh mint leaves

Nutrition facts per 100g:

Calories: 164 kcal
Total Fat: 5.6g
Saturated Fat: 3.2g
Cholesterol: 18mg
Sodium: 107mg
Total Carbohydrate: 24.8g
Dietary Fiber: 2.4g
Sugars: 12.1g
Protein: 6.6g

Preparation:

1. Toast the slices of whole grain bread until golden and crisp.
2. Spread a generous amount of ricotta cheese on each slice of toast.
3. Lay the sliced figs on top of the ricotta, making sure to cover the entire surface.
4. Drizzle honey evenly over the figs.
5. Sprinkle the chopped fresh mint leaves on top.
6. Serve immediately and enjoy your wholesome breakfast!

Chapter 2: Energising Lunches (25 Recipes)

Turkish Lentil Soup (Mercimek Çorbası)

Servings: 4 | Preparation time: 20 minutes

Ingredients

- 200g red lentils
- 1 medium onion, finely chopped
- 2 cloves of garlic, minced
- 2 carrots, finely chopped
- 1 celery stalk, finely chopped
- 1 tablespoon tomato paste
- 1 tablespoon olive oil
- 1 teaspoon ground cumin
- 1 teaspoon paprika
- 1.5 liters vegetable stock
- Juice of 1 lemon
- Salt and pepper, to taste
- Fresh parsley, chopped, for garnish

Nutrition facts per 100g:

Calories: 70
Total Fat: 1g
Saturated Fat: 0g
Trans Fat: 0g
Total Carbohydrate: 12g
Dietary Fiber: 3g
Sugars: 2g
Protein: 4g

Preparation:

1. Rinse the red lentils under cold water until the water runs clear, then set aside.
2. In a large pot, heat the olive oil over medium heat. Add the onion and garlic and sauté until translucent.
3. Add the carrots and celery to the pot and continue to cook for a few minutes until they start to soften.
4. Stir in the tomato paste, cumin, and paprika, and cook for another minute to release their flavours.
5. Add the rinsed lentils to the pot along with the vegetable stock. Bring to a boil, then reduce the heat to low and simmer for about 20 minutes or until the lentils are tender.
6. Using an immersion blender or a regular blender, blend the soup until smooth. If using a regular blender, be sure to allow the soup to cool slightly before blending.
7. Return the soup to the heat and stir in the lemon juice. Season with salt and pepper to taste.
8. Serve the Turkish lentil soup hot, garnished with fresh parsley.

Greek Grilled Chicken & Hummus Wrap

Servings: 4 | Preparation time: 30-40 minutes

Ingredients

- 4 boneless, skinless chicken breasts (approximately 600g)
- 1 tablespoon olive oil
- 2 teaspoons dried oregano
- Juice of 1 lemon
- Salt and pepper, to taste
- 4 whole wheat tortilla wraps
- 200g hummus
- 1 cucumber, thinly sliced
- 2 tomatoes, sliced
- 1 red onion, thinly sliced
- Handful of fresh parsley, chopped

Nutrition facts per 100g:

Calories: 170
Total Fat: 6g
Saturated Fat: 1g
Trans Fat: 0g
Cholesterol: 50mg
Sodium: 200mg
Total Carbohydrate: 13g
Dietary Fiber: 2g
Sugars: 1g
Protein: 16g

Preparation:

1. Preheat your grill or barbecue to medium-high heat. In a bowl, combine the olive oil, dried oregano, lemon juice, salt, and pepper. Mix well.
2. Season the chicken breasts with the prepared marinade, making sure they are well coated. Allow them to marinate for 15-20 minutes.
3. Grill the marinated chicken breasts for approximately 6-8 minutes on each side or until they are cooked through and reach an internal temperature of 75°C.
4. Once cooked, remove the chicken from the grill and allow it to rest for a few minutes. Then, slice the chicken into thin strips.
5. Take one whole wheat tortilla wrap and spread a generous amount of hummus over it.
6. Place a handful of sliced cucumber, tomato, and red onion on top of the hummus.
7. Top with some sliced grilled chicken and sprinkle with fresh parsley.
8. Carefully fold the sides of the tortilla wrap inward and tightly roll it up from one end to the other, keeping all the ingredients inside.
9. Repeat the process with the remaining tortilla wraps and ingredients.
10. Slice each wrap in half diagonally and serve immediately.

Italian Minestrone Soup

Servings: 4 | Preparation time: 30 minutes

Ingredients

- 2 tablespoons extra-virgin olive oil
- 1 onion, finely chopped
- 2 carrots, diced
- 2 celery stalks, diced
- 2 cloves garlic, minced
- 1 zucchini, diced
- 1 cup green beans, cut into 1-inch pieces
- 1 cup cabbage, shredded
- 400g canned chopped tomatoes
- 1 liter vegetable broth
- 1 teaspoon dried oregano
- 1 teaspoon dried thyme
- 1 bay leaf
- 100g small pasta (such as macaroni or orzo)
- Salt and pepper, to taste
- Grated Parmesan cheese, for serving
- Fresh parsley, chopped, for garnish

Nutrition facts per 100g:

Calories: 48
Total Fat: 2g
Saturated Fat: 0g
Trans Fat: 0g
Cholesterol: 0mg
Sodium: 148mg
Total Carbohydrate: 6g
Dietary Fiber: 1g
Sugars: 2g
Protein: 1g

Preparation:

1. In a large pot, heat the olive oil over medium heat. Add the onion, carrots, and celery, and cook until softened, about 5 minutes.
2. Add the garlic, zucchini, green beans, and cabbage, and cook for another 5 minutes.
3. Stir in the chopped tomatoes, vegetable broth, dried oregano, dried thyme, and bay leaf. Bring the soup to a boil, then reduce the heat and let it simmer for 20 minutes.
4. Add the pasta to the pot and cook until al dente, according to the package instructions.
5. Season the soup with salt and pepper to taste.
6. Remove the bay leaf before serving.
7. Ladle the minestrone into bowls. Serve hot, garnished with grated Parmesan cheese and fresh parsley.

Tuna-Stuffed Tomatoes

Servings: 4 | Preparation time: 15 Minutes

Ingredients

- 4 large tomatoes
- 150g canned tuna, drained
- 1 small red onion, finely chopped
- 1 celery stalk, finely chopped
- 2 tablespoons chopped fresh parsley
- 2 tablespoons lemon juice
- 2 tablespoons extra virgin olive oil
- Salt and black pepper, to taste
- 8 black olives, pitted and halved
- Mixed salad greens, for serving

Nutrition facts per 100g:

Calories: 96
Fat: 5.8g
Saturated Fat: 0.9g
Cholesterol: 12mg
Sodium: 233mg
Carbohydrate: 2.9g
Fiber: 0.9g
Sugars: 1.4g
Protein: 8.7g

Preparation:

1. Cut off the tops of the tomatoes and scoop out the seeds and pulp using a spoon. Reserve the tops for later.
2. In a bowl, combine the drained tuna, red onion, celery, parsley, lemon juice, extra virgin olive oil, salt, and black pepper. Mix well until all the ingredients are combined.
3. Stuff the tuna mixture into the hollowed-out tomatoes, gently pressing it down to fill the cavity completely.
4. Place the stuffed tomatoes onto a serving plate and top each with two halved black olives. Replace the tomato tops for an elegant presentation.
5. Serve the tuna-stuffed tomatoes on a bed of mixed salad greens for added freshness and texture.

Mediterranean Couscous Salad

Servings: 4 | Preparation time: 15 minutes

Ingredients

- 250g cherry tomatoes, halved
- 1 cucumber, diced
- 1 red bell pepper, diced
- 1 red onion, finely chopped
- 200g couscous
- 250ml vegetable broth
- 2 tablespoons extra virgin olive oil
- Juice of 1 lemon
- 1 garlic clove, minced
- 1 teaspoon dried oregano
- 1 teaspoon dried basil
- Salt and pepper, to taste
- 50g feta cheese, crumbled
- 30g black olives, pitted and halved
- Fresh parsley, chopped (for garnish)

Nutrition facts per 100g:

Calories: 97 kcal
Total Fat: 3.7g
Saturated Fat: 1.3g
Trans Fat: 0g
Cholesterol: 5mg
Sodium: 91mg
Total Carbohydrate: 12.9g
Dietary Fiber: 1.2g
Sugars: 1.6g
Protein: 2.8g

Preparation:

1. In a large bowl, combine the cherry tomatoes, cucumber, red bell pepper, and red onion. Set aside.
2. In a separate bowl, add the couscous and pour the vegetable broth over it. Cover and let it sit for about 5 minutes, or until all the liquid is absorbed. Fluff the couscous with a fork.
3. In a small bowl, whisk together the olive oil, lemon juice, minced garlic, dried oregano, dried basil, salt, and pepper.
4. Pour the dressing over the vegetable mixture and toss well to combine.
5. Add the cooked couscous to the vegetables and mix until everything is evenly distributed.
6. Sprinkle the crumbled feta cheese and black olives over the salad.
7. Garnish with freshly chopped parsley.
8. Serve immediately or refrigerate for later. This salad can be enjoyed as a light lunch or a side dish.

Greek Salad with Lemon & Oregano Dressing

Servings: 4 | Preparation time: 15 minutes

Ingredients

- 2 large tomatoes, cubed
- 1 cucumber, sliced
- 1 red onion, thinly sliced
- 200g feta cheese, crumbled
- 100g Kalamata olives, pitted
- 1 red bell pepper, diced
- 2 tbsp extra virgin olive oil
- Juice of 1 lemon
- 1 tsp dried oregano
- Salt and pepper to taste

Nutrition facts per 100g:

Calories: 145
Total fat: 11.2g
Saturated fat: 5.2g
Cholesterol: 25mg
Sodium: 388mg
Total carbohydrates: 7.4g
Dietary fiber: 1.8g
Sugars: 3.5g
Protein: 4.6g

Preparation:

1. In a large salad bowl, combine the tomatoes, cucumber, red onion, feta cheese, olives, and red bell pepper.
2. In a small bowl, whisk together the olive oil, lemon juice, dried oregano, salt, and pepper to make the dressing.
3. Pour the dressing over the salad and toss well to coat all the ingredients evenly.
4. Let the salad sit for 10 minutes to allow the flavours to meld together.
5. Serve the Greek salad as a refreshing and energising lunch option.

Warm French Lentil Salad with Dijon Vinaigrette

Servings: 4 | Preparation time: 30 Minutes

Ingredients

- 250g French green lentils
- 1 small red onion, finely chopped
- 1 carrot, finely chopped
- 1 celery stalk, finely chopped
- 1 red bell pepper, finely chopped
- 4 tablespoons extra virgin olive oil
- 2 tablespoons red wine vinegar
- 1 tablespoon Dijon mustard
- 1 clove garlic, minced
- Salt and pepper, to taste
- 2 tablespoons fresh parsley, chopped
- 50g crumbled feta cheese

Nutrition facts per 100g:

Calories: 132
Total Fat: 8g
Saturated Fat: 2g
Total Carbohydrate: 10g
Dietary Fiber: 3g
Sugars: 2g
Protein: 4g

Preparation:

1. Rinse the lentils under cold water and drain them.
2. In a large saucepan, bring 1 liter of water to a boil. Add the lentils and cook for about 20 minutes or until tender. Drain.
3. In a large bowl, combine the cooked lentils, red onion, carrot, celery, and red bell pepper.
4. In a separate small bowl, whisk together the olive oil, red wine vinegar, Dijon mustard, minced garlic, salt, and pepper to make the vinaigrette.
5. Pour the vinaigrette over the lentil mixture and toss to combine.
6. Allow the salad to cool for a few minutes, then sprinkle with chopped parsley and crumbled feta cheese.
7. Serve warm and enjoy.

Stuffed Bell Peppers with Feta Cheese

Servings: 4 | Preparation time: 50 Minutes

Ingredients

- 4 large bell peppers (any color)
- 200g feta cheese, crumbled
- 150g cooked quinoa
- 100g cherry tomatoes, halved
- 1 small red onion, finely chopped
- 1 garlic clove, minced
- 2 tablespoons olive oil
- 1 tablespoon lemon juice
- 1 tablespoon chopped fresh parsley
- Salt and pepper, to taste

Nutrition facts per 100g:

Calories: 135
Total Fat: 9.8g
Saturated Fat: 4.8g
Cholesterol: 25mg
Sodium: 216mg
Total Carbohydrate: 7.9g
Dietary Fiber: 1.5g
Sugars: 3g
Protein: 4.9g

Preparation:

1. Preheat the oven to 200°C (180°C fan).
2. Cut the tops off the bell peppers and remove the seeds and membranes.
3. In a large bowl, mix together the feta cheese, cooked quinoa, cherry tomatoes, red onion, garlic, olive oil, lemon juice, parsley, salt, and pepper.
4. Spoon the filling into the bell peppers, pressing it down lightly.
5. Place the stuffed bell peppers into a baking dish and cover with aluminum foil.
6. Bake for 20 minutes, then remove the foil and bake for an additional 15-20 minutes until the peppers are tender and slightly charred.
7. Serve the stuffed bell peppers warm. They can be enjoyed as a main course or a side dish.

Italian Basil Pesto Pasta

Servings: 4 | Preparation time: 35 minutes

Ingredients

- 400g whole wheat pasta
- 2 cups fresh basil leaves
- 3 cloves garlic, minced
- 1/2 cup grated Parmesan cheese
- 1/2 cup pine nuts, toasted
- 1/2 cup extra virgin olive oil
- Salt and black pepper, to taste
- Cherry tomatoes, halved (for garnish)
- Fresh basil leaves (for garnish)

Nutrition facts per 100g:

Calories: 343 kcal
Total Fat: 22.6g
Saturated Fat: 4.8g
Trans Fat: 0g
Total Carbohydrate: 28.5g
Dietary Fiber: 4.8g
Sugars: 0.6g
Protein: 8.8g

Preparation:

1. Cook the pasta according to package instructions until al dente. Drain and set aside.
2. In a food processor, combine the basil leaves, minced garlic, Parmesan cheese, and toasted pine nuts.
3. Pulse the mixture until everything is well combined and finely chopped.
4. Slowly drizzle in the olive oil through the food processor's feed tube.
5. Continue to process until the mixture becomes a smooth and creamy pesto sauce.
6. Season the pesto sauce with salt and black pepper to taste.
7. In a large mixing bowl, toss the cooked pasta with the basil pesto sauce until evenly coated.
8. Divide the pasta into serving bowls and garnish with halved cherry tomatoes and fresh basil leaves.
9. Serve the Italian Basil Pesto Pasta immediately and enjoy!

Cypriot Halloumi & Watermelon Salad

Servings: 2 | Preparation time: 10 minutes

Ingredients

- 200g halloumi cheese
- 400g watermelon, diced
- 100g cucumber, diced
- 50g red onion, thinly sliced
- 20g fresh mint leaves, chopped
- Juice of 1 lemon
- 2 tablespoons extra virgin olive oil
- Salt and pepper, to taste

Nutrition facts per 100g:

Calories: 142 kcal
Protein: 8.5g
Fat: 10.6g
Saturated fat: 6.9g
Carbohydrates: 4.2g
Fiber: 0.3g
Sugar: 3.1g

Preparation:

1. In a medium-sized bowl, combine the diced watermelon, cucumber, red onion, and chopped mint leaves.
2. In a small bowl, whisk together the lemon juice and olive oil. Season with salt and pepper.
3. Drizzle the dressing over the watermelon mixture and toss gently to combine.
4. Slice the halloumi cheese into 1cm thick pieces.
5. Heat a non-stick frying pan over medium-high heat.
6. Cook the halloumi slices for 2-3 minutes on each side until golden brown.
7. Once cooked, cut the halloumi slices into bite-sized cubes.
8. Add the halloumi cubes to the watermelon salad and gently toss to combine.
9. Serve the Cypriot Halloumi & Watermelon Salad immediately while the halloumi is still warm.

Grilled Eggplant & Red Pepper Sandwich

Servings: 2 | Preparation time: 15-20 minutes

Ingredients

- 1 medium eggplant (about 300g), sliced into 1cm thick rounds
- 1 red pepper, halved and deseeded
- 2 tablespoons olive oil
- 4 slices whole grain bread
- 150g mozzarella cheese, sliced
- Handful of fresh basil leaves
- Salt and pepper, to taste

Nutrition facts per 100g:

Calories: 152
Total fat: 9g
Saturated fat: 3g
Carbohydrate: 13g
Fiber: 5g
Sugars: 6g
Protein: 7g

Preparation:

1. Preheat the grill to medium-high heat.
2. Brush the eggplant slices and red pepper halves with olive oil, season with salt and pepper.
3. Place the eggplant slices and red pepper halves on the grill and cook for about 4-5 minutes per side, until they are tender and slightly charred.
4. Once cooked, remove the eggplant and red pepper from the grill, and set aside to cool slightly.
5. Preheat a pan or griddle over medium heat and lightly oil it.
6. Take two slices of bread and layer each with mozzarella cheese, grilled eggplant slices, grilled red pepper halves, and fresh basil leaves. Season with salt and pepper.
7. Top with the remaining two slices of bread and press gently.
8. Place the sandwiches in the preheated pan or griddle and cook for about 2-3 minutes per side, until the bread is toasted and the cheese has melted.
9. Once cooked, remove the sandwiches from the pan and allow them to cool slightly before serving.

Moroccan Chickpea and Vegetable Stew

Servings: 4 | Preparation time: 40 minutes

Ingredients

- 2 tablespoons olive oil
- 1 onion, finely chopped
- 2 cloves garlic, minced
- 1 teaspoon ground cumin
- 1 teaspoon ground coriander
- 1 teaspoon ground turmeric
- 1 teaspoon smoked paprika
- 1/2 teaspoon ground cinnamon
- 1 carrot, diced
- 1 red bell pepper, diced
- 1 zucchini, diced
- 1 can (400g) chickpeas, drained and rinsed
- 1 can (400g) chopped tomatoes
- 500ml vegetable broth
- Salt and pepper, to taste
- Fresh parsley, for garnish

Nutrition facts per 100g:

Calories: 83
Fat: 3.6g
Saturated Fat: 0.5g
Trans Fat: 0g
Cholesterol: 0mg
Sodium: 202mg
Carbohydrates: 9.8g
Fiber: 2.9g
Sugar: 3.1g
Protein: 2.8g

Preparation:

1. Heat olive oil in a large pot over medium heat. Add the onion and garlic, and sauté until softened.
2. Add the ground cumin, coriander, turmeric, smoked paprika, and cinnamon. Stir well to coat the onions and garlic.
3. Add the diced carrot, red bell pepper, and zucchini to the pot. Cook for about 5 minutes, until the vegetables start to soften.
4. Pour in the chickpeas, chopped tomatoes, and vegetable broth. Season with salt and pepper to taste.
5. Bring the stew to a boil, then reduce the heat to low. Cover and simmer for about 20 minutes, until the vegetables are tender and the flavours have melded together.
6. Serve the Moroccan chickpea and vegetable stew hot, garnished with fresh parsley.

Greek Spinach and Feta Pie (Spanakopita)

Servings: 6 | Preparation time: 35 minutes

Ingredients

- 500g fresh spinach leaves
- 200g feta cheese, crumbled
- 2 tablespoons olive oil
- 1 medium onion, finely chopped
- 3 garlic cloves, minced
- 1 tablespoon fresh dill, chopped
- 1 tablespoon fresh parsley, chopped
- 1 tablespoon fresh mint, chopped
- 4 eggs, beaten
- 6 sheets of filo pastry
- Salt and pepper to taste

Nutrition facts per 100g:

Calories: 155
Total Fat: 10.7g
Saturated Fat: 3.9g
Trans Fat: 0g
Cholesterol: 111mg
Sodium: 377mg
Total Carbohydrate: 8.2g
Dietary Fiber: 1.9g
Sugars: 1.3g
Protein: 7.7g

Preparation:

1. Preheat the oven to 180°C and lightly grease a baking dish.
2. Rinse the spinach leaves thoroughly under cold water and drain.
3. Heat the olive oil in a large pan over medium heat. Add the onions and garlic and sauté until softened and translucent, about 5 minutes.
4. Add the spinach leaves to the pan and cook until wilted, about 2-3 minutes. Remove from heat and set aside to cool.
5. In a mixing bowl, combine the spinach mixture, crumbled feta, beaten eggs, dill, parsley, mint, salt, and pepper. Mix well to ensure even distribution of ingredients.
6. Lay one sheet of filo pastry in the baking dish, allowing it to hang over the edges. Brush with a little olive oil. Repeat with the remaining sheets of filo, brushing each layer with oil before adding the next.
7. Pour the spinach and feta mixture into the baking dish, spreading it evenly.
8. Fold the overhanging filo pastry back over the filling, creating a rustic pie-like shape.
9. Brush the top of the pie with olive oil and bake in the preheated oven for 30-35 minutes or until the top is golden brown.
10. Remove from the oven and allow to cool for a few minutes before slicing and serving.

Tuscan Bean Soup (Ribollita)

Servings: 4 | Preparation time: 1 hour and 50 minutes

Ingredients

- 250g cannellini beans, soaked overnight
- 1 onion, finely chopped
- 2 carrots, diced
- 2 celery stalks, diced
- 2 garlic cloves, minced
- 1 leek, thinly sliced
- 1 bay leaf
- 400g canned chopped tomatoes
- 300g kale, chopped
- 150g stale white bread, torn into chunks
- 1 tablespoon extra virgin olive oil
- Salt and pepper, to taste
- Parmesan cheese, grated for serving

Nutrition facts per 100g:

Calories: 80
Total Fat: 1g
Saturated Fat: 0.2g
Cholesterol: 0mg
Sodium: 160mg
Total Carbohydrate: 15g
Dietary Fiber: 3g
Sugars: 2g
Protein: 4g

Preparation:

1. Drain and rinse the soaked cannellini beans, then place them in a large saucepan with enough water to cover. Bring to a boil and let them simmer gently until tender, around 1 hour. Drain and set aside.
2. In a large soup pot, heat the olive oil over medium heat. Add the onion, carrots, celery, garlic, leek, and bay leaf. Sauté until the vegetables are softened, about 10 minutes.
3. Stir in the canned chopped tomatoes and cooked cannellini beans. Add enough water to cover the vegetables and beans. Bring to a boil, then reduce the heat and simmer for 20 minutes.
4. Add the kale to the pot and cook for an additional 10 minutes, until wilted. Season with salt and pepper to taste.
5. Stir in the torn bread and simmer for another 10 minutes. The bread will thicken the soup and give it a hearty texture.
6. Remove the bay leaf before serving. Ladle the soup into bowls and sprinkle with grated Parmesan cheese.
7. Serve hot and enjoy this delicious and energizing Tuscan Bean Soup for a satisfying lunch option.

Lebanese Falafel Wrap

Servings: 4 | Preparation time: 35-40 minutes

Ingredients

- 400g canned chickpeas, drained
- 1 small onion, roughly chopped
- 2 garlic cloves, minced
- 1 handful fresh parsley leaves
- 1 handful fresh cilantro leaves
- 1 tsp ground cumin
- 1 tsp ground coriander
- 1/2 tsp baking powder
- 4 tbsp plain flour
- Salt and pepper, to taste
- 4 Lebanese flatbreads
- 4 tbsp hummus
- 1 large tomato, thinly sliced
- 1 cucumber, thinly sliced
- 1 small red onion, thinly sliced
- Juice of 1 lemon
- Olive oil, for frying

Nutrition facts per 100g:

Calories: 269
Total Fat: 13g
Saturated Fat: 2g
Trans Fat: 0g
Cholesterol: 0mg
Sodium: 124mg
Total Carbohydrate: 30g
Dietary Fiber: 5g
Sugars: 3g
Protein: 9g

Preparation:

1. In a food processor, combine the chickpeas, onion, garlic, parsley, cilantro, cumin, coriander, baking powder, plain flour, salt, and pepper. Blend until a coarse mixture forms.
2. Transfer the mixture to a bowl and let it rest in the refrigerator for at least half an hour.
3. After chilling, divide the mixture into small patties, about the size of golf balls, and flatten them slightly.
4. Heat some olive oil in a frying pan over medium heat. Fry the falafel patties for 4-5 minutes on each side until golden brown and crispy. Remove from the pan and let them drain on paper towels.
5. Warm the Lebanese flatbreads in a separate dry frying pan or in the oven for a few seconds.
6. To assemble the wraps, spread one tablespoon of hummus on each flatbread, leaving a border around the edges.
7. Place 3-4 falafel patties on top of the hummus, then layer the tomato slices, cucumber slices, and red onion slices on top.
8. Drizzle the lemon juice over the veggies and season with salt and pepper.
9. Roll up the wraps tightly, folding in the edges as you go.
10. Cut the wraps in half diagonally and serve immediately.

Mediterranean Stuffed Pitas

Servings: 4 | Preparation time: 20 Minutes

Ingredients

- 4 wholemeal pitas
- 200g lean chicken breast, cooked and shredded
- 1 small cucumber, diced
- 2 ripe tomatoes, diced
- 1/2 red onion, finely chopped
- 1/2 cup pitted Kalamata olives, halved
- 100g feta cheese, crumbled
- 2 tablespoons extra virgin olive oil
- Juice of 1 lemon
- 1 teaspoon dried oregano
- Salt and pepper to taste

Nutrition facts per 100g:

Calories: 158
Total Fat: 7.5g
Saturated Fat: 1.8g
Trans Fat: 0g
Total Carbohydrate: 12.7g
Dietary Fiber: 2.5g
Sugars: 2.4g
Protein: 11.7g

Preparation:

1. In a large bowl, combine the shredded chicken, diced cucumber, tomatoes, red onion, and Kalamata olives.
2. In a separate small bowl, whisk together the olive oil, lemon juice, dried oregano, salt, and pepper until well combined. This will be the dressing for the filling.
3. Pour the dressing over the chicken and vegetable mixture, and gently toss to coat everything evenly.
4. Carefully cut open each pita pocket to create an opening. Stuff each pita pocket with an equal amount of the chicken and vegetable mixture.
5. Sprinkle the crumbled feta cheese over the top of each stuffed pita.
6. Serve immediately and enjoy this energizing Mediterranean stuffed pita as a delicious and satisfying lunch option.

Moroccan Vegetable Tagine

Servings: 4 | Preparation time: 20-25 minutes

Ingredients

- 2 tablespoons olive oil
- 1 onion, chopped
- 2 cloves garlic, minced
- 1 teaspoon ground cumin
- 1 teaspoon ground coriander
- 1/2 teaspoon ground turmeric
- 1/2 teaspoon ground cinnamon
- 1/4 teaspoon ground ginger
- 1 red bell pepper, sliced
- 2 carrots, peeled and chopped
- 1 small sweet potato, peeled and diced
- 1 can (400g) chopped tomatoes
- 250ml vegetable broth
- 200g chickpeas, cooked
- 100g dried apricots, chopped
- Zest and juice of 1 lemon
- Salt and pepper to taste
- Fresh coriander leaves, for garnish
- Cooked couscous or quinoa, for serving

Nutrition facts per 100g:

Calories: 81
Total Fat: 2g
Saturated Fat: 0.3g
Cholesterol: 0mg
Sodium: 141mg
Total Carbohydrate: 13g
Dietary Fiber: 4g
Sugars: 5g
Protein: 3g

Preparation:

1. Heat olive oil in a large pot over medium heat. Add chopped onion and minced garlic, and sauté until translucent.
2. Add ground cumin, coriander, turmeric, cinnamon, and ginger to the pot. Stir well to coat the onions and garlic with the spices.
3. Add sliced red bell pepper, chopped carrots, and diced sweet potato to the pot. Cook for a few minutes until the vegetables start to soften.
4. Pour in the chopped tomatoes and vegetable broth. Bring to a gentle simmer and let it cook for 15-20 minutes, or until vegetables are tender.
5. Stir in the cooked chickpeas and dried apricots. Cook for an additional 5 minutes to allow the flavours to meld together.
6. Add the lemon zest and juice to the pot, and season with salt and pepper to taste.
7. Serve the Moroccan vegetable tagine hot over cooked couscous or quinoa. Garnish with fresh coriander leaves.

Traditional Greek Souvlaki

Servings: 4 | Preparation time: 50-60 minutes

Ingredients

- 500g boneless chicken breasts, cut into bite-sized pieces
- 1 large red onion, sliced
- Juice of 1 lemon
- 4 tablespoons olive oil
- 2 tablespoons dried oregano
- 2 garlic cloves, minced
- Salt and pepper, to taste
- 4 pita breads
- Tzatziki sauce, for serving
- Chopped fresh parsley, for garnish

Nutrition facts per 100g:

Calories: 160 kcal
Total Fat: 7 g
Saturated Fat: 1.5 g
Trans Fat: 0 g
Total Carbohydrate: 7 g
Dietary Fiber: 0.75 g
Sugar: 1.5 g
Protein: 18 g

Preparation:

1. In a large bowl, combine the lemon juice, olive oil, dried oregano, minced garlic, salt, and pepper. Mix well to create a marinade.
2. Add the chicken pieces to the marinade and toss until they are evenly coated. Cover the bowl with plastic wrap and let the chicken marinate in the fridge for at least 30 minutes, or up to overnight.
3. Preheat a grill or skillet over medium-high heat.
4. Thread the marinated chicken pieces onto skewers, alternating with slices of red onion.
5. Place the skewers on the grill or skillet, and cook for about 10-12 minutes, turning occasionally, until the chicken is cooked through and slightly charred.
6. While the chicken is cooking, warm the pita breads in a toaster or on the grill for a few seconds on each side.
7. Once the chicken is ready, remove it from the skewers and divide it equally among the warmed pita breads.
8. Serve the souvlaki with a generous drizzle of tzatziki sauce and a sprinkle of chopped fresh parsley.

Italian Antipasti Platter

Servings: 4 | Preparation time: 15 minutes

Ingredients

- 100g cherry tomatoes, halved
- 150g mozzarella balls, drained
- 100g prosciutto, thinly sliced
- 100g salami, sliced
- 100g mixed olives
- 1 small cucumber, sliced
- 1 red bell pepper, sliced
- 1 yellow bell pepper, sliced
- 4 artichoke hearts, sliced
- 4 sun-dried tomatoes, sliced
- Handful of fresh basil leaves
- Extra virgin olive oil, for drizzling
- Balsamic glaze, for drizzling
- Salt and black pepper, to taste

Nutrition facts per 100g:

Calories: 180
Total Fat: 11g
Saturated Fat: 5g
Total Carbohydrate: 4g
Dietary Fiber: 1g
Sugars: 1g
Protein: 13g

Preparation:

1. Arrange the cherry tomatoes, mozzarella balls, prosciutto, salami, mixed olives, cucumber, bell peppers, artichoke hearts, sun-dried tomatoes, and fresh basil leaves on a large serving platter.
2. Drizzle the platter with extra virgin olive oil and balsamic glaze.
3. Season with salt and black pepper to taste.
4. Serve immediately and enjoy as a light and energizing lunch.

Greek Lemon Rice (Avgolemono)

Servings: 4 | Preparation time: 30 minutes

Ingredients

- 200g long-grain white rice
- 4 cups vegetable stock
- 2 lemons, juice and zest
- 2 medium eggs
- 1 tablespoon extra-virgin olive oil
- Salt, to taste
- Freshly ground black pepper, to taste
- Fresh parsley, for garnish

Nutrition facts per 100g:

Calories: 112
Fat: 3g
Saturated Fat: 0.6g
Carbohydrates: 19g
Fiber: 0.7g
Sugar: 0.6g
Protein: 3g

Preparation:

1. In a large saucepan, bring the vegetable stock to a boil. Add the rice and cook according to package instructions until tender. Remove from heat and set aside.
2. In a bowl, whisk together the lemon juice, lemon zest, and eggs until well combined.
3. Slowly pour the lemon and egg mixture into the cooked rice, stirring constantly to avoid curdling the eggs.
4. Return the saucepan to low heat and cook the rice, stirring gently, for a few more minutes until the dish thickens slightly.
5. Drizzle the extra-virgin olive oil over the rice and season with salt and freshly ground black pepper to taste.
6. Remove from heat and let the dish cool for a few minutes before serving.
7. Garnish with fresh parsley and serve warm as a refreshing and energizing lunch option.

Turkish Bulgur and Lentil Soup

Servings: 4 | Preparation time: 20 minutes

Ingredients

- 150 grams bulgur
- 150 grams red lentils
- 1 onion, finely chopped
- 2 cloves of garlic, minced
- 1 carrot, diced
- 1 potato, diced
- 1 tomato, chopped
- 1 tablespoon tomato paste
- 1 teaspoon paprika
- 1 teaspoon cumin
- 1 teaspoon dried oregano
- 1 bay leaf
- 1.5 liters vegetable or chicken stock
- Juice of 1 lemon
- Salt and pepper, to taste
- Fresh parsley, chopped (for garnish)
- Olive oil (for drizzling)

Nutrition facts per 100g:

Calories: 98
Total Fat: 1.4g
Saturated Fat: 0.2g
Total Carbohydrate: 17.6g
Dietary Fiber: 5.1g
Sugars: 1.6g
Protein: 5.2g

Preparation:

1. Rinse the red lentils and bulgur in a sieve until the water runs clear.
2. In a large pot, heat some olive oil over medium heat and sauté the onion and garlic until fragrant and translucent.
3. Add the carrot, potato, and tomato to the pot and cook for a few minutes until slightly softened.
4. Stir in the tomato paste, paprika, cumin, dried oregano, and bay leaf. Cook for another minute.
5. Add the red lentils, bulgur, and vegetable or chicken stock to the pot. Bring to a boil, then reduce the heat and simmer for about 20 minutes or until the lentils and bulgur are cooked through and tender.
6. Remove the bay leaf and season the soup with salt, pepper, and lemon juice.
7. Use an immersion blender or transfer a portion of the soup to a blender and blitz until smooth. Add the blended soup back into the pot and stir well.
8. Serve the Turkish Bulgur and Lentil Soup hot, garnished with fresh parsley, and drizzle with olive oil.

Spanish Tomato Bread (Pan con Tomate)

Servings: 4 | Preparation time: 10 minutes

Ingredients

- 4 slices of crusty bread
- 4 ripe tomatoes
- 2 garlic cloves, peeled
- Extra virgin olive oil, for drizzling
- Sea salt, to taste

Nutrition facts per 100g:

Calories: 167
Total Fat: 6.4g
Saturated Fat: 1g
Cholesterol: 0mg
Sodium: 247mg
Total Carbohydrate: 23.7g
Dietary Fiber: 2.7g
Sugars: 4.4g
Protein: 3.8g

Preparation:

1. Slice the tomatoes in half and grate them on the large side of a box grater into a bowl. Discard the skins.
2. Toast the bread slices until golden and crispy.
3. While the bread is still hot, rub each slice with a garlic clove. The heat will help release the garlic's flavour.
4. Spoon the grated tomatoes over the garlic-rubbed bread slices, ensuring they are evenly distributed.
5. Drizzle each slice with a generous amount of extra virgin olive oil.
6. Sprinkle sea salt over the tomato-topped bread slices, according to your taste preference.
7. Serve the Spanish tomato bread immediately as a light lunch or a tasty snack.

Provençal Ratatouille with Fresh Herbs

Servings: 4 | Preparation time: 25 minutes

Ingredients

- 2 tablespoons olive oil
- 1 onion, sliced
- 2 cloves garlic, minced
- 1 red bell pepper, sliced
- 1 yellow bell pepper, sliced
- 1 medium-sized eggplant, diced
- 2 zucchinis, sliced
- 4 tomatoes, diced
- 2 tablespoons tomato paste
- 1 teaspoon dried thyme
- 1 teaspoon dried oregano
- 1 bay leaf
- Salt and pepper to taste
- Fresh basil leaves, chopped
- Fresh parsley leaves, chopped

Nutrition facts per 100g:

Calories: 64
Total fat: 3.5g
Saturated fat: 0.5g
Total carbohydrate: 8g
Dietary fiber: 3g
Sugars: 5g
Protein: 1g

Preparation:

1. Heat the olive oil in a large pan over medium heat.
2. Add the onion and garlic to the pan and cook until the onion becomes translucent, about 3 minutes.
3. Add the red and yellow bell peppers to the pan. Cook for another 3 minutes until they start to soften.
4. Add the eggplant and zucchinis to the pan and cook for 5 minutes until they begin to brown slightly.
5. Stir in the diced tomatoes and tomato paste. Mix well to combine.
6. Season the mixture with dried thyme, dried oregano, bay leaf, salt, and pepper. Stir to evenly distribute the herbs and spices.
7. Reduce the heat to low, cover the pan, and let the ratatouille simmer for 20-25 minutes until all the vegetables are tender and flavours have melded.
8. Remove the bay leaf from the pan and adjust salt and pepper to taste.
9. Serve the Provençal Ratatouille hot, garnished with fresh chopped basil and parsley leaves.

Sicilian Caponata

Servings: 4 | Preparation time: 30 minutes

Ingredients

- 3 tablespoons olive oil
- 1 medium eggplant, cubed
- 1 red bell pepper, sliced
- 1 yellow bell pepper, sliced
- 1 red onion, sliced
- 2 celery stalks, sliced
- 3 garlic cloves, minced
- 400 grams canned chopped tomatoes
- 2 tablespoons tomato paste
- 2 tablespoons red wine vinegar
- 1 tablespoon capers
- 8 green olives, pitted and halved
- 2 tablespoons raisins
- 1 teaspoon sugar
- Salt and pepper, to taste
- Fresh basil leaves, chopped, for garnish

Nutrition facts per 100g:

Calories: 101
Total fat: 6g
Saturated fat: 1g
Cholesterol: 0mg
Sodium: 223mg
Total carbohydrates: 11g
Dietary fiber: 4g
Sugars: 6g
Protein: 2g

Preparation:

1. In a large frying pan, heat 2 tablespoons of olive oil over medium heat. Add the eggplant and cook until golden brown and tender. Remove the eggplant from the pan and set aside.
2. In the same pan, add the remaining tablespoon of olive oil. Add the red and yellow bell peppers, red onion, celery, and garlic. Sauté until the vegetables are softened.
3. Add the canned chopped tomatoes, tomato paste, red wine vinegar, capers, olives, raisins, sugar, salt, and pepper to the pan. Stir well to combine.
4. Reduce the heat to low and simmer the mixture for about 15 minutes, or until the flavours have melded together.
5. Add the cooked eggplant back to the pan and stir gently to combine all the ingredients.
6. Allow the caponata to cool slightly before serving. Garnish with fresh chopped basil leaves.
7. Serve the Sicilian Caponata warm or at room temperature as a side dish or over crusty bread for a light lunch or appetizer.

Mediterranean Avocado Salad

Servings: 2 | Preparation time: 10-15 minutes

Ingredients

- 2 ripe avocados
- 200g cherry tomatoes
- 1 cucumber
- 100g feta cheese
- 1 small red onion
- 2 tablespoons extra virgin olive oil
- Juice of 1 lemon
- Salt, to taste
- Pepper, to taste
- Fresh basil leaves, for garnish

Nutrition facts per 100g:

Calories: 157
Total Fat: 13.4g
Saturated Fat: 4.1g
Cholesterol: 16mg
Sodium: 280mg
Total Carbohydrate: 7.4g
Dietary Fiber: 3.9g
Sugars: 2.8g
Protein: 4.6g

Preparation:

1. Cut the avocados in half, remove the pit, and slice them into thin wedges. Place the avocado slices in a large serving bowl.
2. Halve the cherry tomatoes and add them to the bowl.
3. Peel the cucumber, cut it in half lengthwise, and slice it. Add the cucumber slices to the bowl.
4. Finely chop the red onion and crumble the feta cheese. Add them to the bowl.
5. Drizzle the extra virgin olive oil and lemon juice over the salad.
6. Season with salt and pepper according to your taste.
7. Gently toss all the ingredients together until well combined.
8. Transfer the salad to individual plates or a serving platter.
9. Garnish with fresh basil leaves.
10. Serve immediately as a light and energising Mediterranean-inspired lunch.

Chapter 3: Satisfying Dinners (30 Recipes)

Greek Moussaka with Lamb and Aubergine

Servings: 6 | Preparation time: 1 hour

Ingredients

- 500g lamb mince
- 2 large aubergines
- 1 onion, finely chopped
- 3 garlic cloves, minced
- 400g tinned chopped tomatoes
- 2 tbsp tomato puree
- 1 tsp dried oregano
- 1 tsp dried thyme
- 1 tsp ground cinnamon
- Salt and pepper, to taste
- 4 tbsp olive oil
- 50g plain flour
- 500ml milk
- 50g butter
- 50g grated Parmesan cheese

Nutrition facts per 100g:

Calories: 185
Total Fat: 11g
Saturated Fat: 4g
Trans Fat: 0g
Cholesterol: 35mg
Sodium: 208mg
Total Carbohydrate: 10g
Dietary Fiber: 2g
Sugars: 5g
Protein: 12g

Preparation:

1. Preheat the oven to 200°C (180°C fan).
2. Slice the aubergines into rounds, approximately 1cm thick. Arrange them on a baking tray and drizzle with 2 tablespoons of olive oil. Bake for 15-20 minutes until golden brown.
3. In a large frying pan, heat 2 tablespoons of olive oil over medium heat. Add the onion and garlic and cook until softened.
4. Add the lamb mince to the pan and cook until browned. Stir in the tomato puree, dried herbs, and cinnamon. Season with salt and pepper and cook for another 5 minutes.
5. Pour in the tinned chopped tomatoes and simmer for 15 minutes, allowing the flavours to meld together.
6. In a separate saucepan, melt the butter over low heat. Add the flour and cook for 1 minute, stirring constantly. Gradually pour in the milk, whisking continuously, and cook until the sauce thickens.
7. Remove the saucepan from the heat and stir in half of the grated Parmesan cheese. Season with salt and pepper.
8. In a greased baking dish, layer half of the aubergines at the bottom. Spoon the lamb mixture on top, followed by another layer of aubergines. Pour the white sauce evenly over the top.
9. Sprinkle the remaining Parmesan cheese on top and bake in the preheated oven for 30-35 minutes, until golden and bubbling.
10. Allow the moussaka to cool for a few minutes before serving.

Seafood Paella Valenciana

Servings: 4 | Preparation time: 45 minutes

Ingredients

- 400g paella rice
- 700ml fish or vegetable stock
- 500g mixed seafood (such as prawns, mussels, and squid)
- 1 onion, finely chopped
- 2 garlic cloves, minced
- 1 red bell pepper, diced
- 1 ripe tomato, diced
- 150g green beans, trimmed and halved
- 1 teaspoon smoked paprika
- A pinch of saffron threads
- 2 tablespoons olive oil
- Salt and pepper, to taste
- Fresh parsley, chopped (for garnish)
- Lemon wedges (for serving)

Nutrition facts per 100g:

Calories: 105 g
Protein: 7 g
Fat: 2 g
Carbohydrates: 16 g
Fiber: 0.6 g

Preparation:

1. Heat the olive oil in a large, shallow paella pan over medium heat. Add the onion, garlic, and red bell pepper. Sauté for about 5 minutes until softened.
2. Stir in the diced tomato, smoked paprika, and saffron threads. Cook for another 2 minutes.
3. Add the rice to the pan and stir well until it is evenly coated with the tomato mixture.
4. Pour in the stock and bring to a simmer. Cook gently for about 15 minutes, stirring occasionally.
5. Meanwhile, prepare the seafood by cleaning and deveining the prawns, scrubbing the mussels, and slicing the squid into rings.
6. After 15 minutes, add the green beans and seafood to the pan. Season with salt and pepper. Gently stir everything together.
7. Cover the pan with a lid or aluminum foil and cook for another 10 minutes, or until the rice is tender and the seafood is cooked through.
8. Once done, remove from heat and let it rest, covered, for a few minutes.
9. Serve the seafood paella valenciana garnished with chopped parsley and lemon wedges on the side.

Italian Baked Cod with Tomatoes and Olives

Servings: 4 | Preparation time: 35 Minutes

Ingredients

- 4 cod fillets (about 150g each)
- 400g cherry tomatoes, halved
- 100g pitted Kalamata olives
- 2 cloves garlic, minced
- 2 tablespoons olive oil
- 2 tablespoons freshly squeezed lemon juice
- 1 teaspoon dried oregano
- Salt and pepper, to taste
- Fresh basil leaves, for garnish

Nutrition facts per 100g:

Calories: 109
Total Fat: 4.8g
Saturated Fat: 0.7g
Trans Fat: 0g
Total Carbohydrate: 4.7g
Dietary Fiber: 1.3g
Sugars: 2g
Protein: 12.7g

Preparation:

1. Preheat the oven to 200°C (180°C fan).
2. In a large baking dish, combine the cherry tomatoes, olives, minced garlic, olive oil, lemon juice, dried oregano, salt, and pepper. Toss everything together until well coated.
3. Place the cod fillets on top of the tomato and olive mixture in the baking dish.
4. Season the cod fillets with salt, pepper, and a drizzle of olive oil.
5. Cover the baking dish with foil and bake in the preheated oven for 15 minutes.
6. Remove the foil, increase the oven temperature to 220°C (200°C fan), and bake for an additional 5-10 minutes or until the cod is cooked through and flakes easily with a fork.
7. Garnish the baked cod with fresh basil leaves.
8. Serve the Italian Baked Cod with Tomatoes and Olives accompanied by your choice of side dishes or with crusty bread.

Moroccan Lamb Tagine with Apricots

Servings: 4 | Preparation time: 1 hour

Ingredients

- 500g lamb shoulder, diced
- 2 tablespoons olive oil
- 1 onion, finely chopped
- 2 cloves of garlic, minced
- 1 teaspoon ground cumin
- 1 teaspoon ground coriander
- 1 teaspoon ground turmeric
- 1 teaspoon ground cinnamon
- 1 teaspoon paprika
- 1/2 teaspoon ground ginger
- 1/2 teaspoon chili powder (optional, for heat)
- 400g canned chopped tomatoes
- 250ml lamb or vegetable stock
- 150g dried apricots, halved
- Handful of fresh coriander, chopped (for garnish)
- Salt and pepper, to taste

Nutrition facts per 100g:

Calories: 175
Total Fat: 9g
Saturated Fat: 3g
Total Carbohydrate: 12g
Dietary Fiber: 2g
Sugars: 9g
Protein: 12g

Preparation:

1. Heat the olive oil in a large, heavy-bottomed casserole dish over medium heat. Add the lamb shoulder and cook until browned on all sides. Remove the lamb from the dish and set aside.
2. In the same casserole dish, add the onion and garlic. Sauté until softened and lightly golden.
3. Add the ground cumin, coriander, turmeric, cinnamon, paprika, ginger, and chili powder (if using). Stir well to coat the onions and garlic.
4. Return the lamb to the dish, along with any juices, and add the chopped tomatoes and lamb or vegetable stock. Season with salt and pepper to taste. Stir to combine all the ingredients.
5. Bring the mixture to a boil, then reduce the heat to low and cover the dish. Allow the tagine to simmer for about 1 hour, or until the lamb is tender.
6. Stir in the dried apricots and continue simmering for another 10 minutes, until the apricots have softened and infused the dish with their sweetness.
7. Serve the Moroccan lamb tagine hot, garnished with freshly chopped coriander. This dish pairs perfectly with couscous or crusty bread.

Ratatouille Stuffed Zucchini Boats

Servings: 4 | Preparation time: 45 minutes

Ingredients

- 4 medium zucchinis
- 2 tablespoons olive oil
- 1 small onion, finely chopped
- 2 cloves garlic, minced
- 1 red bell pepper, diced
- 1 yellow bell pepper, diced
- 1 small eggplant, diced
- 2 medium tomatoes, diced
- 1 teaspoon dried oregano
- Salt and pepper, to taste
- 1/4 cup grated Parmesan cheese
- Fresh basil leaves, for garnish

Nutrition facts per 100g:

Calories: 58
Total Fat: 3.9g
Saturated Fat: 1.1g
Cholesterol: 2mg
Sodium: 83mg
Total Carbohydrate: 4.9g
Dietary Fiber: 1.2g
Sugars: 2.4g
Protein: 1.9g

Preparation:

1. Preheat the oven to 200°C.
2. Cut the zucchinis in half lengthwise and scoop out the flesh, leaving about 1/4-inch-thick shell. Reserve the flesh.
3. Heat the olive oil in a large skillet over medium heat. Add the onion and garlic and sauté until they become translucent.
4. Add the bell peppers, eggplant, and reserved zucchini flesh to the skillet and cook until the vegetables soften, around 5 minutes.
5. Stir in the tomatoes, dried oregano, salt, and pepper. Cook for another 5 minutes, allowing the flavours to blend.
6. Arrange the zucchini boats in a baking dish and spoon the ratatouille mixture into each boat.
7. Sprinkle the grated Parmesan cheese evenly over the boats.
8. Bake in the preheated oven for 20-25 minutes, or until the zucchinis are tender and the cheese is golden and bubbly.
9. Remove from the oven and let them cool slightly. Garnish with fresh basil leaves before serving.

Lebanese Lentils, Rice and Caramelised Onions (Mujadara)

Servings: 4 | Preparation time: 45 minutes

Ingredients

- 200g green or brown lentils
- 200g basmati rice
- 3 large onions, thinly sliced
- 4 tablespoons olive oil, divided
- 1 teaspoon ground cumin
- 1 teaspoon ground coriander
- 1 teaspoon ground cinnamon
- Salt and black pepper, to taste
- Fresh parsley, for garnish

Nutrition facts per 100g:

Calories: 130
Total Fat: 6g
Saturated Fat: 1g
Cholesterol: 0mg
Sodium: 200mg
Total Carbohydrate: 16g
Dietary Fiber: 5g
Sugars: 2g
Protein: 4g

Preparation:

1. Rinse the lentils and place them in a saucepan with 500ml of water. Bring to a boil, then reduce the heat and simmer for about 15-20 minutes, or until the lentils are tender. Drain any excess water.
2. In a separate saucepan, cook the rice according to the package instructions. Once cooked, set aside.
3. Heat 2 tablespoons of olive oil in a large skillet over medium heat. Add the sliced onions and cook, stirring occasionally, until soft and golden brown, about 15-20 minutes.
4. Remove half of the caramelized onions from the skillet and set aside for garnishing.
5. To the skillet with the remaining onions, add the cooked lentils, ground cumin, ground coriander, ground cinnamon, salt, and black pepper. Stir well to combine and allow the flavours to meld for a few minutes.
6. In a separate small pan, heat the remaining 2 tablespoons of olive oil over medium heat. Add the reserved caramelized onions and cook for a few minutes until they are crispy. Remove from the pan and set aside.
7. To serve, spoon the mujadara (lentils and rice mixture) onto serving plates. Top with a generous amount of the caramelized onions that were set aside for garnishing. Sprinkle with fresh parsley and crispy onions.
8. This Lebanese lentils, rice, and caramelized onions dish, known as Mujadara, can be enjoyed as a hearty vegetarian main course or served alongside grilled meats and vegetables for a complete meal.

Greek Style Baked Chicken Souvlaki

Servings: 4 | Preparation time: 75 minutes

Ingredients

- 4 chicken breasts, boneless and skinless (around 600g)
- 4 tablespoons extra virgin olive oil
- Juice of 2 lemons
- 4 garlic cloves, minced
- 2 teaspoons dried oregano
- 1 teaspoon dried thyme
- Salt and black pepper, to taste
- 4 pita breads
- Tzatziki sauce, to serve
- Diced tomatoes, cucumber, and red onion, for garnish

Nutrition facts per 100g:

Calories: 196
Protein: 20.1g
Carbohydrates: 5.6g
Fat: 10.6g
Saturated Fat: 1.7g
Fiber: 0.7g
Sugar: 0.5g
Sodium: 158mg

Preparation:

1. Preheat your oven to 200°C (180°C fan). Line a baking sheet with parchment paper.
2. In a bowl, combine the olive oil, lemon juice, minced garlic, oregano, thyme, salt, and black pepper.
3. Cut the chicken breasts into bite-sized chunks and add them to the bowl with the marinade. Make sure the chicken is well coated. Let it marinate for at least 30 minutes or refrigerate overnight for more flavour.
4. Thread the marinated chicken pieces onto skewers, discarding any excess marinade.
5. Place the skewers on the prepared baking sheet and bake for 20-25 minutes, or until the chicken is cooked through and nicely browned.
6. While the chicken is baking, warm the pita bread in the oven for a few minutes.
7. Once the chicken is cooked, remove it from the skewers and serve on the warmed pita breads.
8. Top with a dollop of tzatziki sauce and garnish with diced tomatoes, cucumber, and red onion.
9. Serve hot and enjoy your Greek-style baked chicken souvlaki.

Italian Chicken Cacciatore

Servings: 4 | Preparation time: 30 minutes

Ingredients

- 4 chicken thighs, bone-in and skin-on (about 900g)
- 1 tablespoon olive oil
- 1 medium onion, finely chopped
- 2 cloves of garlic, minced
- 1 red bell pepper, sliced
- 1 yellow bell pepper, sliced
- 200g mushrooms, sliced
- 200g cherry tomatoes, halved
- 1 tablespoon tomato puree
- 200ml chicken stock
- 100ml red wine
- 1 teaspoon dried oregano
- 1 teaspoon dried basil
- Salt and pepper, to taste
- Fresh parsley, for garnish

Nutrition facts per 100g:

Calories: 132
Total fat: 5.6g
Saturated fat: 1.4g
Cholesterol: 54mg
Sodium: 212mg
Total carbohydrates: 5.8g
Dietary fiber: 1.3g
Sugars: 2.8g
Protein: 10.8g

Preparation:

1. Season the chicken thighs with salt and pepper.
2. Heat the olive oil in a large, deep skillet over medium-high heat. Add the chicken thighs and cook until golden brown on both sides. Remove from the skillet and set aside.
3. In the same skillet, add the onion, garlic, and bell peppers. Sauté for 5 minutes or until the vegetables have softened.
4. Add the mushrooms and cherry tomatoes to the skillet. Cook for another 5 minutes, until the mushrooms have released their juices.
5. Stir in the tomato puree, chicken stock, red wine, oregano, and basil. Bring to a simmer.
6. Return the chicken thighs to the skillet, making sure they are submerged in the sauce. Reduce the heat to low, cover, and simmer for 30 minutes, or until the chicken is cooked through and tender.
7. Serve the chicken cacciatore hot, garnished with fresh parsley.

Shrimp Saganaki with Ouzo

Servings: 4 | Preparation time: 30 minutes

Ingredients

- 500g shrimp, peeled and deveined
- 1 onion, finely chopped
- 2 garlic cloves, minced
- 400g canned tomatoes
- 50ml ouzo
- 100g feta cheese, crumbled
- 2 tablespoons olive oil
- 1 teaspoon dried oregano
- Salt and pepper to taste
- Fresh parsley, chopped (for garnish)

Nutrition facts per 100g:

Calories: 145
Total Fat: 8g
Saturated Fat: 3g
Trans Fat: 0g
Cholesterol: 132mg
Sodium: 310mg
Total Carbohydrate: 5g
Dietary Fiber: 1g
Sugars: 3g
Protein: 13g

Preparation:

1. Heat olive oil in a large pan over medium heat. Add the chopped onion and sauté until translucent.
2. Stir in the minced garlic and cook for an additional minute.
3. Pour in the canned tomatoes and break them apart with a spoon. Season with salt, pepper, and dried oregano. Simmer for about 15 minutes, until the sauce thickens slightly.
4. Add the shrimp to the pan and cook for about 2-3 minutes until they turn pink and opaque.
5. Carefully pour in the ouzo and flambe the shrimp. Watch out for any flames and be cautious.
6. Crumble the feta cheese over the pan and cover with a lid. Allow the cheese to melt over low heat for another 2-3 minutes.
7. Give the dish a gentle stir to combine the ingredients and ensure the cheese is evenly distributed.
8. Remove from heat and garnish with fresh parsley.
9. Serve warm over a bed of rice or with crusty bread for dipping.

Turkish Imam Bayildi (Stuffed Eggplants)

Servings: 4 | Preparation time: 1 hour

Ingredients

- 4 small eggplants (about 250g each)
- 4 tablespoons olive oil, divided
- 1 small onion, finely chopped
- 2 cloves garlic, minced
- 1 red bell pepper, finely chopped
- 2 tomatoes, finely chopped
- 2 tablespoons tomato paste
- 1 teaspoon sugar
- 1/2 teaspoon dried oregano
- 1/2 teaspoon dried thyme
- Salt and pepper to taste
- 1/4 cup fresh parsley, chopped
- 1/4 cup fresh mint, chopped
- Lemon wedges, for serving

Nutrition facts per 100g:

Calories: 105
Total Fat: 7.4g
Saturated Fat: 1.0g
Trans Fat: 0g
Total Carbohydrate: 10g
Dietary Fiber: 4g
Sugars: 4.9g
Protein: 2g

Preparation:

1. Preheat the oven to 200°C (180°C fan).
2. Cut each eggplant in half lengthwise and scoop out the flesh, leaving about 1-centimeter thick shells. Chop the scooped-out flesh and set aside.
3. Heat 2 tablespoons of olive oil in a large skillet over medium heat. Add the onion and garlic, cooking until softened and fragrant.
4. Add the red bell pepper and chopped eggplant flesh. Cook for 5 minutes until they start to soften.
5. Stir in the tomatoes, tomato paste, sugar, dried oregano, dried thyme, salt, and pepper. Cook for an additional 5 minutes.
6. Remove from heat and stir in the fresh parsley and mint.
7. Brush the eggplant shells with the remaining olive oil and place them in a baking dish. Fill each shell with the vegetable mixture.
8. Cover the baking dish with foil and bake for 30 minutes.
9. Remove the foil and continue baking for an additional 10 minutes or until the eggplants are tender and slightly browned.
10. Serve hot with lemon wedges on the side.

Italian Osso Buco with Gremolata

Servings: 4 | Preparation time: 3 hours

Ingredients

- 4 veal shanks (about 1.2 kg), bone-in
- 4 tablespoons plain flour
- Salt and black pepper, to season
- 3 tablespoons olive oil
- 1 onion, finely chopped
- 2 carrots, finely chopped
- 2 celery stalks, finely chopped
- 3 garlic cloves, minced
- 2 sprigs fresh rosemary
- 2 bay leaves
- 250 ml dry white wine
- 400 g chopped tomatoes
- 500 ml beef stock

Nutrition facts per 100g:

Calories: 148 kcal
Protein: 15.4g
Carbohydrates: 7.8g
Fat: 5.1g
Fiber: 1.1g
Sodium: 226mg

For the Gremolata:

- Zest of 1 lemon
- 2 garlic cloves, minced
- 2 tablespoons fresh parsley, finely chopped

Preparation:

1. Preheat the oven to 180°C.
2. Season the veal shanks with salt and black pepper, then dust them with flour, shaking off any excess.
3. Heat the olive oil in a large ovenproof casserole dish over medium-high heat. Sear the veal shanks until browned on all sides. Remove and set aside.
4. In the same dish, add the onion, carrots, celery, and garlic. Sauté for 5 minutes until softened.
5. Add the rosemary sprigs, bay leaves, white wine, chopped tomatoes, and beef stock. Bring to a simmer.
6. Return the veal shanks to the dish, ensuring they are submerged in the liquid. Cover and transfer to the preheated oven.
7. Cook for 2 to 2.5 hours, or until the meat is tender and falling off the bone.
8. In a small bowl, combine the lemon zest, minced garlic, and chopped parsley to prepare the gremolata.
9. Once the veal shanks are cooked, remove them from the dish and skim off any excess fat from the sauce if desired.
10. Serve the osso buco with the sauce, sprinkled with gremolata on top. Accompany with your desired side dish, such as creamy polenta or risotto.

Lebanese Kibbeh with Ground Beef and Pine Nuts

Servings: 4 | Preparation time: 45 minutes

Ingredients

- 500g ground beef
- 200g bulgur wheat
- 1 onion, finely minced
- 2 garlic cloves, minced
- 3 tablespoons pine nuts
- 2 teaspoons ground cumin
- 1 teaspoon ground coriander
- 1/2 teaspoon ground cinnamon
- 1/4 teaspoon cayenne pepper
- Salt, to taste
- Olive oil, for frying

Nutrition facts per 100g:

Calories: 230
Protein: 14g
Fat: 14g
Carbohydrate: 14g
Fiber: 2g
Sugar: 1g
Sodium: 150mg

Preparation:

1. Place the bulgur wheat in a bowl and cover it with water. Let it soak for 10 minutes, then drain the excess water and set aside.
2. In a large mixing bowl, combine the ground beef, minced onion, minced garlic, soaked bulgur wheat, cumin, coriander, cinnamon, cayenne pepper, and salt. Mix well until all the ingredients are evenly combined.
3. In a small frying pan, heat a drizzle of olive oil over medium heat. Add the pine nuts and cook until lightly toasted and fragrant. Remove from heat and set aside.
4. Take a small portion of the beef mixture and shape it into an oblong-shaped patty. Make a hole in the center using your thumb, making sure the walls are about 1/4-inch thick.
5. Fill the hole with a teaspoon of the toasted pine nuts, then gently close the edges, shaping it back into an oblong shape. Repeat with the remaining mixture.
6. Heat some olive oil in a large frying pan over medium heat. Add the kibbeh patties and cook for about 4-5 minutes per side, or until golden brown and cooked through.
7. Serve the Lebanese kibbeh hot with a side of yogurt, fresh herbs, and a squeeze of lemon juice, if desired.

Greek Lemon and Garlic Roasted Potatoes

Servings: 4 | Preparation time: 45 minutes

Ingredients

- 1 kg potatoes (cut into wedges)
- 4 tablespoons olive oil
- 4 cloves garlic (minced)
- 2 lemons (juiced)
- 1 teaspoon dried oregano
- Salt and pepper to taste
- Fresh parsley (chopped, for garnish)

Nutrition facts per 100g:

Calories: 144
Total Fat: 6.8g
Saturated Fat: 1g
Trans Fat: 0g
Cholesterol: 0mg
Sodium: 3mg
Total Carbohydrate: 19.9g
Dietary Fiber: 2.6g
Sugars: 1.5g
Protein: 2.2g

Preparation:

1. Preheat the oven to 200°C (180°C fan).
2. In a large mixing bowl, combine the olive oil, minced garlic, lemon juice, dried oregano, salt, and pepper.
3. Add the potato wedges to the bowl and toss until evenly coated with the mixture.
4. Transfer the potatoes to a baking tray, spreading them out in a single layer.
5. Roast the potatoes in the preheated oven for 40-45 minutes, or until they are golden brown and crispy.
6. Stir the potatoes occasionally during cooking to prevent sticking.
7. Once cooked, remove the potatoes from the oven and garnish with freshly chopped parsley.
8. Serve hot and enjoy as a side dish or as a satisfying vegetarian main course.

Sardinian Seafood Pasta with Saffron

Servings: 4 | Preparation time: 20 minutes

Ingredients

- 300g pasta (e.g., spaghetti or linguine)
- 500g mixed seafood (such as prawns, mussels, and squid)
- 1 pinch of saffron threads
- 2 tablespoons olive oil
- 1 small red onion, finely chopped
- 2 cloves garlic, minced
- 1 can (400g) chopped tomatoes
- 100ml white wine
- 1 lemon, zested and juiced
- Salt and pepper, to taste
- Fresh parsley, chopped, for garnish

Nutrition facts per 100g:

Calories: 120
Total Fat: 5g
Saturated Fat: 1g
Trans Fat: 0g
Total Carbohydrate: 10g
Dietary Fiber: 1g
Sugars: 2g
Protein: 10g

Preparation:

1. Bring a large pot of salted water to a boil and cook the pasta according to the package instructions until al dente. Drain and set aside.
2. In a small bowl, steep the saffron threads in a tablespoon of hot water and set aside.
3. Heat the olive oil in a large pan over medium heat. Add the chopped onion and minced garlic and cook until softened and fragrant.
4. Add the mixed seafood to the pan and cook for about 3 minutes, or until they start to turn opaque. Remove the seafood from the pan and set aside.
5. In the same pan, add the chopped tomatoes, white wine, saffron (along with the water it was steeped in), lemon zest, and juice. Season with salt and pepper to taste. Cook for about 10 minutes, allowing the flavours to meld together.
6. Add the cooked seafood back into the pan and simmer for another 3-5 minutes until heated through.
7. Toss the cooked pasta into the seafood sauce, ensuring it's well coated. Cook for an additional minute or two to allow the pasta to absorb the flavours.
8. Divide the Sardinian seafood pasta among serving plates. Garnish with freshly chopped parsley and additional lemon zest if desired.
9. Serve immediately and enjoy this delightful taste of Sardinia.

Tunisian Couscous with Lamb and Vegetables

Servings: 4 | Preparation time: 1.5 hours

Ingredients

- 300g lamb shoulder, diced
- 1 tablespoon olive oil
- 1 onion, finely chopped
- 2 garlic cloves, minced
- 1 teaspoon ground cumin
- 1 teaspoon ground coriander
- 1 teaspoon ground turmeric
- 1 teaspoon paprika
- 1 cinnamon stick
- 400g canned chopped tomatoes
- 400g canned chickpeas, drained and rinsed
- 500ml vegetable stock
- 200g couscous
- 200g mixed vegetables (such as carrots, zucchini, and bell peppers), diced
- Salt and pepper, to taste
- Fresh cilantro, chopped, for garnish

Nutrition facts per 100g:

Calories: 120 kcal
Total Fat: 4 g
Total Carbohydrate: 13 g
Fiber: 2 g
Sugars: 2 g
Protein: 8 g

Preparation:

1. Heat the olive oil in a large pan and add the diced lamb. Cook until browned on all sides, then remove from the pan and set aside.
2. In the same pan, add the chopped onion and minced garlic. Sauté until softened.
3. Add the ground cumin, ground coriander, ground turmeric, paprika, and cinnamon stick. Cook for a minute until fragrant.
4. Return the lamb to the pan and add the canned chopped tomatoes, drained chickpeas, and vegetable stock. Season with salt and pepper.
5. Bring the mixture to a simmer, then cover and cook for about 1 hour or until the lamb is tender and the flavours have melded together.
6. In the meantime, prepare the couscous according to the package instructions.
7. After the lamb has cooked for an hour, add the mixed vegetables to the pan. Cover and cook for an additional 10-15 minutes until the vegetables are tender.
8. Fluff the cooked couscous with a fork and serve with the lamb and vegetable stew on top.
9. Garnish with freshly chopped cilantro.

Italian Eggplant Parmigiana

Servings: 4 | Preparation time: 35 minutes

Ingredients

- 2 large eggplants (about 800 grams)
- 400 grams of tinned chopped tomatoes
- 200 grams of mozzarella cheese, grated
- 50 grams of Parmesan cheese, grated
- 2 cloves of garlic, minced
- 1 tablespoon of olive oil
- 1 teaspoon of dried oregano
- Salt and pepper, to taste
- Fresh basil leaves, for garnish

Nutrition facts per 100g:

Calories: 113 kcal
Total Fat: 6.9 g
Saturated Fat: 3.9 g
Cholesterol: 18 mg
Sodium: 239 mg
Total Carbohydrate: 6.6 g
Dietary Fiber: 2.3 g
Sugars: 3.4 g
Protein: 6.2 g

Preparation:

1. Preheat the oven to 200°C (180°C fan). Line a baking tray with parchment paper.
2. Slice the eggplants into 1 cm thick rounds. Sprinkle salt over each slice and set them aside in a colander for 15 minutes to release excess moisture.
3. Rinse the eggplant slices under cold water to remove the salt and pat them dry with a kitchen towel.
4. Heat the olive oil in a large frying pan over medium heat. Add the minced garlic and cook until fragrant, about 1 minute.
5. Add the tinned chopped tomatoes and dried oregano to the pan. Stir well and let it simmer for 10-15 minutes until the sauce thickens. Season with salt and pepper to taste.
6. Meanwhile, preheat a grill pan over high heat. Cook the eggplant slices in batches until nicely charred on both sides, approximately 2-3 minutes per side. Transfer the grilled slices to the prepared baking tray.
7. Spoon a layer of tomato sauce onto each eggplant slice. Sprinkle grated mozzarella and Parmesan cheese over the sauce.
8. Repeat the process, layering the eggplant, sauce, and cheese until all the ingredients are used.
9. Bake in the preheated oven for 20-25 minutes until the cheese is melted and golden brown.
10. Garnish with fresh basil leaves before serving.

Cypriot Chicken Souvla with Tzatziki

Servings: 4 | Preparation time: 20-25 minutes

Ingredients

- 1.5 kg chicken thighs, bone-in and skin-on
- 6 large garlic cloves, crushed
- Juice of 1 lemon
- 3 tablespoons olive oil
- 1 teaspoon dried oregano
- 1 teaspoon dried thyme
- 1 teaspoon smoked paprika
- Salt and pepper, to taste

For the Tzatziki:

- 1 medium cucumber, grated
- 1 cup Greek yogurt
- 2 cloves garlic, minced
- 2 tablespoons fresh dill, chopped
- 1 tablespoon olive oil
- Salt and pepper, to taste

Nutrition facts per 100g:

Calories: 208 kcal
Total Fat: 13g
Saturated Fat: 3g
Cholesterol: 79mg
Sodium: 34mg
Carbohydrates: 2g
Fiber: 0g
Sugars: 1g
Protein: 21g

Preparation:

1. In a large bowl, combine the crushed garlic, lemon juice, olive oil, dried oregano, dried thyme, smoked paprika, salt, and pepper. Mix well to create a marinade.
2. Add the chicken thighs to the marinade, ensuring they are coated evenly. Cover the bowl with plastic wrap and refrigerate for at least 2 hours or overnight for maximum flavour.
3. Preheat the grill to medium-high heat.
4. Remove the chicken thighs from the marinade and thread them onto skewers, leaving a small gap between each piece.
5. Grill the chicken skewers for about 15-20 minutes, turning occasionally, until the chicken is cooked through and nicely charred.
6. Meanwhile, prepare the tzatziki. In a bowl, combine the grated cucumber, Greek yogurt, minced garlic, fresh dill, olive oil, salt, and pepper. Mix well.
7. Serve the chicken souvla hot off the grill with the tzatziki sauce on the side.

Moroccan Vegetable and Chickpea Couscous

Servings: 4 | Preparation time: 25 minutes

Ingredients

- 250g couscous
- 1 tablespoon olive oil
- 1 onion, finely chopped
- 2 garlic cloves, minced
- 1 red bell pepper, diced
- 1 zucchini, diced
- 2 carrots, diced
- 1 teaspoon ground cumin
- 1 teaspoon ground paprika
- ½ teaspoon ground turmeric
- 400g tin of chickpeas, drained and rinsed
- 400g tin of chopped tomatoes
- 500ml vegetable stock
- Handful of fresh parsley, chopped
- Salt and pepper, to taste

Nutrition facts per 100g:

Calories: 97 kcal
Total Fat: 1.9g
Saturated Fat: 0.3g
Trans Fat: 0g
Cholesterol: 0mg
Sodium: 251mg
Total Carbohydrate: 17.5g
Dietary Fiber: 3.4g
Sugars: 3.9g
Protein: 3.9g

Preparation:

1. Place the couscous in a large bowl and pour boiling water over it until it's just covered. Set it aside for about 10 minutes or until the water is absorbed.
2. Heat the olive oil in a large saucepan over medium heat. Add the onion and garlic, and sauté until softened.
3. Add the red bell pepper, zucchini, and carrots to the pan. Cook for about 5 minutes, stirring occasionally.
4. Stir in the cumin, paprika, and turmeric, and cook for another minute or until fragrant.
5. Add the chickpeas, chopped tomatoes, and vegetable stock to the pan. Bring it to a boil, then reduce the heat to low and simmer for 15 minutes.
6. Fluff the couscous with a fork and add it to the pan. Stir well to combine.
7. Season with salt and pepper to taste and cook for another 5 minutes to allow the flavours to meld together.
8. Serve the Moroccan vegetable and chickpea couscous hot, garnished with fresh parsley.

Greek Baked Fish with Tomatoes and Onions (Psari Plaki)

Servings: 4 | Preparation time: 35 minutes

Ingredients

- 4 white fish fillets (such as cod or haddock), 150g each
- 400g cherry tomatoes, halved
- 1 red onion, thinly sliced
- 2 cloves of garlic, minced
- 2 tablespoons extra virgin olive oil
- 1 tablespoon tomato paste
- 2 tablespoons fresh lemon juice
- 1 teaspoon dried oregano
- 1 teaspoon dried thyme
- Salt and pepper, to taste
- Fresh parsley, chopped for garnish

Nutrition facts per 100g:

Calories: 125
Protein: 15g
Fat: 4g
Carbohydrates: 8g
Fiber: 2g

Preparation:

1. Preheat the oven to 200°C.
2. Place the fish fillets in a baking dish.
3. In a separate bowl, combine cherry tomatoes, red onion, garlic, olive oil, tomato paste, lemon juice, dried oregano, dried thyme, salt, and pepper. Mix well to coat the tomatoes and onions with the seasonings.
4. Spoon the tomato and onion mixture over the fish fillets.
5. Cover the baking dish with foil and bake for 15 minutes.
6. Remove the foil and bake for an additional 10 minutes or until the fish is cooked through and flakes easily with a fork.
7. Once cooked, remove from the oven and let it rest for a few minutes.
8. Sprinkle with fresh parsley for garnish.
9. Serve the Greek baked fish hot as a main course, accompanied by steamed vegetables, a side of couscous, or crusty bread.

Spanish Chorizo and Potato Stew

Servings: 4 | Preparation time: 20-25 minutes

Ingredients

- 2 tablespoons olive oil
- 200g Spanish chorizo, sliced
- 1 onion, finely chopped
- 2 garlic cloves, minced
- 500g new potatoes, diced
- 1 red pepper, diced
- 1 can (400g) chopped tomatoes
- 2 bay leaves
- 1 teaspoon smoked paprika
- 500ml chicken or vegetable broth
- Salt and pepper, to taste
- Fresh parsley, for garnish

Nutrition facts per 100g:

Calories: 146
Protein: 5.6g
Carbohydrates: 12.4g
Fat: 8.5g
Saturated Fat: 2.8g
Fiber: 2.4g
Sugar: 2.4g
Sodium: 389mg

Preparation:

1. In a large pan, heat the olive oil over medium-high heat. Add the chorizo slices and cook until they release their oils and turn crispy. Remove from pan and set aside.
2. In the same pan, add the chopped onion and minced garlic. Sauté for 2-3 minutes until fragrant and translucent.
3. Add the diced potatoes and red pepper to the pan. Cook for another 5 minutes, stirring occasionally.
4. Pour in the can of chopped tomatoes and add the bay leaves and smoked paprika. Season with salt and pepper to your liking. Stir everything together.
5. Pour in the chicken or vegetable broth and bring the stew to a boil. Reduce heat, cover, and let it simmer for about 20 minutes or until the potatoes are tender.
6. Once the stew is ready, stir in the cooked chorizo slices. Allow it to simmer for an additional 5 minutes to let the flavours combine.
7. Remove the bay leaves and discard. Serve the Spanish Chorizo and Potato Stew in bowls, garnished with fresh parsley.

Lebanese Chicken and Rice (Riz bi-Djaj)

Servings: 4 | Preparation time: 25 minutes

Ingredients

- 500g boneless chicken thighs, cut into bite-sized pieces
- 2 tablespoons olive oil
- 1 large onion, finely chopped
- 2 cloves garlic, minced
- 1 teaspoon ground cumin
- 1 teaspoon ground cinnamon
- 1 teaspoon ground turmeric
- 1 cup basmati rice
- 2 cups chicken broth
- Salt and black pepper, to taste
- 2 tablespoons chopped fresh parsley
- Lemon wedges, for serving

Nutrition facts per 100g:

Calories: 150 kcal
Protein: 10 g
Fat: 6 g
Carbohydrates: 14 g
Fiber: 0.5 g
Sugar: 1 g
Sodium: 120 mg

Preparation:

1. In a large frying pan or skillet, heat the olive oil over medium heat. Add the chopped onion and cook until softened and slightly browned, about 5 minutes.
2. Add the minced garlic, ground cumin, ground cinnamon, and ground turmeric to the pan. Stir well to combine and cook for another minute.
3. Add the chicken pieces to the pan and cook until browned on all sides, about 5 minutes.
4. Stir in the basmati rice, ensuring it is evenly coated with the spices and juices from the chicken.
5. Pour in the chicken broth and season with salt and black pepper. Bring to a boil, then reduce the heat to low, cover, and simmer for 15 minutes or until the rice is cooked and the liquid has been absorbed.
6. Remove the pan from heat and let it sit, covered, for another 5 minutes to allow the flavours to meld and the rice to fluff up.
7. Just before serving, sprinkle with chopped parsley and serve with lemon wedges on the side for squeezing over the dish.

Greek Stuffed Tomatoes and Peppers (Gemista)

Servings: 4 | Preparation time: 1 hour

Ingredients

- 4 large tomatoes
- 4 bell peppers (assorted colors)
- 1 cup cooked rice
- 1 small onion, finely chopped
- 2 cloves of garlic, minced
- 1/2 cup chopped fresh parsley
- 1/4 cup chopped fresh mint
- 1/4 cup chopped fresh dill
- 1/4 cup olive oil, plus extra for drizzling
- 1 tablespoon tomato paste
- Juice of 1 lemon
- Salt and pepper to taste

Nutrition facts per 100g:

Calories: 102
Total Fat: 4.4g
Saturated Fat: 0.6g
Trans Fat: 0g
Cholesterol: 0mg
Sodium: 64mg
Total Carbohydrate: 14.7g
Dietary Fiber: 2.5g
Sugars: 6.1g
Protein: 1.9g

Preparation:

1. Preheat your oven to 180°C.
2. Cut the tops off the tomatoes and peppers and set aside. Scoop out the pulp and seeds from the tomatoes and hollow out the peppers.
3. In a large bowl, combine the rice, onion, garlic, parsley, mint, dill, olive oil, tomato paste, lemon juice, salt, and pepper. Mix well.
4. Stuff the tomatoes and peppers with the rice mixture, filling them to the top.
5. Place the stuffed tomatoes and peppers in a baking dish. Drizzle olive oil over the top.
6. Place the reserved tops on the tomatoes and peppers.
7. Cover the baking dish with foil and bake for 30 minutes.
8. Remove the foil and bake for an additional 15-20 minutes, or until the tomatoes and peppers are tender and slightly golden on top.
9. Serve hot as a delicious main dish.

Italian Pasta alla Norma

Servings: 4 | Preparation time: 25 minutes

Ingredients

- 320g dried penne pasta
- 3 tablespoons olive oil
- 1 small onion, finely chopped
- 2 garlic cloves, minced
- 400g tin chopped tomatoes
- 2 medium-sized aubergines, cut into small cubes
- Salt, to taste
- Black pepper, to taste
- 1 teaspoon dried oregano
- 70g ricotta salata or grated pecorino cheese
- Fresh basil leaves, for garnish

Nutrition facts per 100g:

Calories: 152
Protein: 4g
Fat: 7g
Saturated fat: 2g
Carbohydrates: 18g
Fiber: 2g
Sugar: 2g
Sodium: 127mg

Preparation:

1. Cook the penne pasta according to package instructions, until al dente. Drain and set aside.
2. In a large frying pan, heat the olive oil over medium heat. Add the onion and garlic, and sauté until fragrant and golden.
3. Add the chopped tomatoes to the pan and stir well. Simmer for 5 minutes to allow the flavours to meld.
4. Meanwhile, in a separate frying pan, heat a little more olive oil over medium-high heat. Add the cubed aubergines and stir-fry until they are golden brown and softened.
5. Transfer the cooked aubergines to the tomato sauce, and season with salt, black pepper, and dried oregano. Stir well and simmer for another 10 minutes.
6. Add the cooked penne pasta to the sauce and toss until evenly coated.
7. Divide the pasta alla Norma among serving plates. Crumble the ricotta salata or sprinkle pecorino cheese over the top.
8. Garnish each plate with a few fresh basil leaves. Serve immediately and enjoy!

Portuguese Piri Piri Chicken

Servings: 4 | Preparation time: 25 minutes

Ingredients

- 4 boneless, skin-on chicken breasts (about 600g)
- 2 tablespoons olive oil
- 4 garlic cloves, minced
- 2 tablespoons fresh lemon juice
- 2 tablespoons red wine vinegar
- 2 tablespoons sweet paprika
- 1 tablespoon smoked paprika
- 1 teaspoon dried oregano
- 1 teaspoon dried thyme
- 1 teaspoon salt
- 1 teaspoon black pepper
- 1-2 bird's eye chilies, finely chopped (adjust according to spice preference)
- Fresh parsley, chopped (for garnish)

Nutrition facts per 100g:

Calories: 210 kcal
Total Fat: 12g
Saturated Fat: 3g
Cholesterol: 60mg
Sodium: 350mg
Total Carbohydrate: 4g
Fiber: 1g
Sugar: 1g
Protein: 22g

Preparation:

1. In a large mixing bowl, combine the olive oil, minced garlic, lemon juice, red wine vinegar, paprika (both sweet and smoked), oregano, thyme, salt, black pepper, and bird's eye chilies. Mix well to form a homogeneous marinade.
2. Place the chicken breasts in the marinade, making sure they're fully coated. Cover and refrigerate for at least 2 hours, or overnight for maximum flavour.
3. Preheat your grill or barbecue to medium-high heat.
4. Remove the chicken from the marinade, allowing any excess marinade to drip off.
5. Grill the chicken breasts for about 5-7 minutes on each side, or until they reach an internal temperature of 165°C (75°C) and the juices run clear.
6. Once cooked, transfer the chicken to a serving platter and allow it to rest for a few minutes.
7. Garnish with fresh chopped parsley and serve the Portuguese Piri Piri Chicken with your choice of sides or a green salad.

Tunisian Harissa-spiced Chicken

Servings: 4 | Preparation time: 45 minutes

Ingredients

- 4 chicken thighs, bone-in and skin-on
- 2 tablespoons harissa paste
- 1 tablespoon olive oil
- 2 cloves garlic, minced
- 1 teaspoon ground cumin
- 1 teaspoon ground coriander
- 1 teaspoon paprika
- 1/2 teaspoon salt
- Freshly ground black pepper
- Juice of 1/2 lemon
- Fresh cilantro, chopped (for garnish)

Nutrition facts per 100g:

Calories: 204
Total Fat: 13g
Saturated Fat: 3g
Cholesterol: 67mg
Sodium: 410mg
Total Carbohydrate: 1g
Dietary Fiber: 0g
Sugars: 0g
Protein: 20g

Preparation:

1. Preheat the oven to 200°C.
2. In a small bowl, mix together the harissa paste, olive oil, minced garlic, ground cumin, ground coriander, paprika, salt, and black pepper.
3. Place the chicken thighs in a baking dish and spread the harissa mixture over the chicken, ensuring it is evenly coated.
4. Squeeze the juice of half a lemon over the chicken.
5. Bake the chicken in the preheated oven for 30-35 minutes, or until the chicken is cooked through and the skin is crispy.
6. Once cooked, remove the chicken from the oven and let it rest for a few minutes.
7. Serve the Tunisian harissa-spiced chicken with a sprinkle of fresh cilantro on top.

Italian Pork Scaloppine with Lemon

Servings: 4 | Preparation time: 10 minutes

Ingredients

- 600g pork tenderloin
- 100g all-purpose flour
- Salt and pepper, to taste
- 2 tablespoons olive oil
- 2 cloves garlic, minced
- 120ml chicken or vegetable broth
- 60ml white wine
- Juice of 2 lemons
- 1 tablespoon capers
- 2 tablespoons fresh parsley, chopped
- Lemon wedges, for serving

Nutrition facts per 100g:

Calories: 171
Total Fat: 9.7g
Saturated Fat: 2.4g
Cholesterol: 55mg
Sodium: 356mg
Total Carbohydrate: 5.6g
Dietary Fiber: 0.4g
Total Sugars: 0.5g
Protein: 14.1g

Preparation:

1. Slice the pork tenderloin into thin medallions, about 1cm thick. Place a piece of plastic wrap over the medallions and gently pound them with a meat mallet until they're even thinner, about 0.5cm thick.
2. In a shallow dish, mix the flour with salt and pepper. Dredge the pork slices in the flour mixture, shaking off any excess.
3. Heat the olive oil in a large pan over medium-high heat. Cook the pork slices in batches until they're golden brown on both sides, about 2 minutes per side. Remove the cooked slices from the pan and set them aside on a plate.
4. In the same pan, add the minced garlic and cook for about 30 seconds until fragrant. Pour in the broth, white wine, and lemon juice. Bring the mixture to a simmer and let it cook for 3-4 minutes until slightly reduced.
5. Add the capers and half of the chopped parsley to the pan. Stir well to combine.
6. Return the pork slices to the pan and cook for an additional 2-3 minutes, allowing them to soak up the flavours of the sauce.
7. Serve the Italian pork scaloppine with lemon hot, garnished with the remaining parsley and lemon wedges on the side.

Sicilian Swordfish with Olives and Capers

Servings: 4 | Preparation time: 25 minutes

Ingredients

- 500g swordfish steaks
- 200g cherry tomatoes, halved
- 100g pitted green olives
- 50g capers, drained
- 2 garlic cloves, minced
- 2 tablespoons extra virgin olive oil
- 1 lemon, zest and juice
- 1 tablespoon fresh parsley, chopped
- Salt and black pepper, to taste

Nutrition facts per 100g:

Calories: 148
Protein: 19g
Fat: 7g
Carbohydrates: 3g
Fiber: 1g

Preparation:

1. Preheat the oven to 200°C.
2. In a baking dish, place the swordfish steaks and season with salt and black pepper.
3. In a bowl, combine the cherry tomatoes, olives, capers, garlic, olive oil, lemon zest, and lemon juice. Mix well.
4. Pour the tomato and olive mixture over the swordfish steaks, ensuring they are evenly coated.
5. Place the baking dish in the preheated oven and bake for 20-25 minutes, or until the fish is cooked through and flakes easily with a fork.
6. While the swordfish is baking, periodically spoon the sauce over the fish to keep it moist and flavourful.
7. Once cooked, remove the baking dish from the oven and sprinkle the chopped parsley over the top.
8. Serve the Sicilian swordfish hot, with a side of steamed vegetables or a salad, and enjoy!

Spanish Lentil and Chorizo Stew

Servings: 4 | Preparation time: 50 minutes

Ingredients

- 200g chorizo sausages, sliced
- 1 onion, diced
- 2 cloves of garlic, minced
- 2 carrots, diced
- 2 celery stalks, diced
- 200g green lentils
- 400g canned chopped tomatoes
- 500ml vegetable stock
- 1 tsp smoked paprika
- 1 tsp dried oregano
- Salt and pepper, to taste
- Fresh parsley, chopped (for garnish)

Nutrition facts per 100g:

Calories: 171
Total Fat: 8.2g
Saturated Fat: 2.9g
Total Carbohydrate: 14.8g
Dietary Fiber: 2.8g
Sugars: 2.9g
Protein: 8.6g

Preparation:

1. In a large pot, cook the chorizo slices over medium heat for 3-4 minutes or until slightly crispy. Remove them from the pot and set aside, leaving the flavourful oil in the pot.
2. Add the diced onion to the pot and cook for 3-4 minutes until softened. Stir in the minced garlic, carrots, and celery, and cook for another 2 minutes.
3. Add the lentils, canned chopped tomatoes, vegetable stock, smoked paprika, and dried oregano to the pot. Stir well to combine.
4. Bring the stew to a boil, then reduce the heat, cover, and simmer for about 30-40 minutes or until the lentils are tender, stirring occasionally.
5. Season with salt and pepper according to taste.
6. Serve the stew hot, garnished with the cooked chorizo slices and chopped parsley.

Greek Baked Gigantes Beans

Servings: 4 | Preparation time: 60 minutes

Ingredients

- 400g dried gigantes beans
- 1 carrot, peeled and diced
- 1 celery stalk, diced
- 1 onion, diced
- 3 garlic cloves, minced
- 400g canned chopped tomatoes
- 2 tablespoons tomato paste
- 1 tablespoon dried oregano
- 1 teaspoon ground cumin
- Salt and pepper, to taste
- 50g feta cheese, crumbled
- Fresh parsley, for garnish

Nutrition facts per 100g:

Calories: 108 kcal
Protein: 6 g
Fat: 2 g
Carbohydrates: 18 g
Fiber: 7 g
Sugar: 3 g
Sodium: 105 mg

Preparation:

1. Soak the gigantes beans overnight in water. Drain and rinse them the next day.
2. Preheat the oven to 180°C.
3. In a large pot, bring salted water to a boil and cook the gigantes beans for 45-60 minutes until tender. Drain and set aside.
4. In a separate pan, heat some olive oil and sauté the carrot, celery, onion, and garlic until softened.
5. Stir in the canned chopped tomatoes, tomato paste, dried oregano, ground cumin, salt, and pepper. Cook for about 5 minutes.
6. Add the cooked gigantes beans to the tomato mixture and combine well.
7. Transfer the mixture to an ovenproof dish and cover it with foil. Bake for 45 minutes.
8. Remove the foil, sprinkle the crumbled feta cheese on top, and bake for an additional 10 minutes until the cheese is slightly melted.
9. Remove from the oven and let it rest for a few minutes.
10. Garnish with fresh parsley and serve hot.

Lebanese Spinach and Beef Stew (Sabzi Polo)

Servings: 4 | Preparation time: 1 hour

Ingredients

- 500g beef stew meat, cut into cubes
- 2 tablespoons olive oil
- 1 onion, chopped
- 3 garlic cloves, minced
- 500g spinach leaves, washed and chopped
- 1 teaspoon ground cumin
- 1 teaspoon ground coriander
- 1 teaspoon ground cinnamon
- 1 teaspoon salt
- ½ teaspoon black pepper
- 400ml beef or vegetable stock
- 250g long-grain rice
- Fresh parsley, chopped (for garnish)
- Lemon wedges (for serving)

Nutrition facts per 100g:

Calories: 123
Total Fat: 4.5g
Saturated Fat: 1.2g
Trans Fat: 0g
Cholesterol: 31mg
Sodium: 374mg
Total Carbohydrate: 9.7g
Dietary Fiber: 1.7g
Sugars: 0.9g
Protein: 11.2g

Preparation:

1. In a large pot, heat olive oil over medium heat. Add the beef cubes and cook until browned on all sides. Remove the beef from the pot and set aside.
2. In the same pot, add the chopped onion and minced garlic. Sauté until the onion becomes soft and translucent.
3. Add the spinach leaves to the pot and cook until wilted, stirring occasionally.
4. Return the beef to the pot and add the ground cumin, coriander, cinnamon, salt, and black pepper. Stir well to coat the beef and spinach with the spices.
5. Pour in the beef or vegetable stock and bring to a boil. Reduce the heat to low, cover the pot, and simmer for 1 hour, or until the beef is tender.
6. Meanwhile, rinse the rice under cold water until the water runs clear. Cook the rice according to package instructions.
7. Serve the Lebanese Spinach and Beef Stew over a bed of cooked rice. Garnish with fresh parsley and serve with lemon wedges for squeezing.

Chapter 4: Light Bites and Snacks (20 Recipes)

Mediterranean Stuffed Mini Peppers

Servings: 4 | Preparation time: 15 minutes

Ingredients

- 12 mini bell peppers (around 200g)
- 150g feta cheese, crumbled
- 50g black olives, pitted and chopped
- 2 tablespoons fresh parsley, chopped
- 1 tablespoon fresh lemon juice
- 1 tablespoon olive oil
- Salt and pepper, to taste

Nutrition facts per 100g:

Energy: 156 calories
Protein: 7.2g
Carbohydrates: 6.8g
Fat: 11.1g
Fiber: 1.5g
Sodium: 493mg

Preparation:

1. Preheat the oven to 200°C (180°C fan/400°F/gas mark 6) and line a baking tray with parchment paper.
2. Slice the tops off the mini bell peppers, then carefully remove the seeds and membranes, creating small hollows.
3. In a mixing bowl, combine the crumbled feta, chopped black olives, fresh parsley, lemon juice, and olive oil. Season with salt and pepper to taste.
4. Spoon the feta mixture into the hollowed mini peppers, pressing it gently to fill them evenly.
5. Place the stuffed peppers on the prepared baking tray and bake in the preheated oven for 12-15 minutes or until the peppers are tender and lightly browned.
6. Once cooked, remove from the oven and allow to cool for a few minutes before serving.

Greek Dolmades (Stuffed Vine Leaves)

Servings: 20 dolmades | Preparation time: 45 minutes

Ingredients

- 200g vine leaves, preserved in brine
- 200g long-grain rice
- 1 small onion, finely chopped
- 2 tablespoons fresh parsley, finely chopped
- 2 tablespoons fresh dill, finely chopped
- 2 tablespoons fresh mint, finely chopped
- 1 tablespoon lemon juice
- 2 tablespoons olive oil
- Salt and pepper, to taste

Nutrition facts per 100g:

Calories: 151
Protein: 2.2g
Fat: 4.5g
Carbohydrates: 26.4g
Fiber: 0.8g
Sugar: 0.6g
Sodium: 576mg

Preparation:

1. Rinse the preserved vine leaves under cold water to remove excess salt, then place them in a large bowl with warm water and let them soak for 10 minutes. Drain and pat them dry with kitchen paper.
2. In a separate bowl, soak the rice in cold water for 5 minutes, then drain.
3. In a pan, heat olive oil over medium heat and add the chopped onion. Cook for 3-4 minutes until softened.
4. Add the drained rice to the pan and stir well to coat it with the onion and oil mixture. Cook for 2 minutes.
5. Pour in 400ml of water and bring the mixture to a simmer. Reduce the heat, cover the pan, and let it cook for 10-12 minutes until the rice is tender and the water is absorbed. Remove from heat and let it cool slightly.
6. Add the chopped parsley, dill, mint, lemon juice, salt, and pepper to the rice mixture. Stir until well combined.
7. Lay a vine leaf flat on a clean surface, shiny side down, and place a spoonful of the rice mixture in the center of the leaf. Fold the bottom of the leaf up over the filling, then fold in the sides, and roll it tightly into a small parcel. Repeat with the remaining vine leaves and filling.
8. Arrange the dolmades on a serving plate and serve as a light snack or appetizer. They can be enjoyed at room temperature or chilled.

Olive Tapenade Crostini

Servings: 6 | Preparation time: 45 minutes

Ingredients

- 200g black olives, pitted
- 30g capers
- 1 garlic clove, minced
- 2 tablespoons fresh parsley, chopped
- 2 tablespoons fresh basil, chopped
- 1 tablespoon lemon juice
- 2 tablespoons extra virgin olive oil
- Salt and black pepper, to taste
- 1 baguette, sliced into rounds and toasted

Nutrition facts per 100g:

Calories: 212
Total Fat: 21g
Saturated Fat: 3g
Cholesterol: 0mg
Sodium: 726mg
Total Carbohydrate: 5g
Dietary Fiber: 3g
Sugars: 0.5g
Protein: 1g

Preparation:

1. In a food processor, combine the black olives, capers, minced garlic, parsley, basil, lemon juice, and extra virgin olive oil. Pulse until well combined but still slightly chunky.
2. Taste the mixture and season with salt and black pepper according to your preference.
3. Transfer the olive tapenade to a bowl and cover it. Place it in the refrigerator for at least 30 minutes to allow the flavours to meld together.
4. Take the toasted baguette rounds and spread a generous amount of the olive tapenade on each slice.
5. Arrange the crostini on a platter and serve immediately. These can be enjoyed as a light snack or appetizer.

Greek Tzatziki with Vegetable Crudites

Servings: Approximately 6 servings | Preparation time: 20 minutes

Ingredients

- 500g Greek yoghurt
- 1 large cucumber (about 300g), grated and excess water squeezed out
- 2 cloves of garlic, minced
- 1 tablespoon extra-virgin olive oil
- 1 tablespoon lemon juice
- 1 tablespoon fresh dill, chopped
- Salt, to taste
- Freshly ground black pepper, to taste
- Assorted vegetable crudites (e.g., carrots, celery, bell peppers, cherry tomatoes)

Nutrition facts per 100g:

Calories: 83
Total Fat: 5g
Saturated Fat: 2.8g
Cholesterol: 15mg
Sodium: 36mg
Total Carbohydrate: 3.3g
Dietary Fiber: 0.2g
Sugars: 2.5g
Protein: 6.3g

Preparation:

1. In a large bowl, combine the Greek yoghurt, grated cucumber, minced garlic, olive oil, lemon juice, and chopped dill.
2. Mix well until all the ingredients are evenly incorporated.
3. Season with salt and freshly ground black pepper to taste.
4. Transfer the tzatziki to a serving bowl and cover it. Refrigerate for at least an hour to allow the flavours to meld together.
5. Meanwhile, prepare the vegetable crudites by washing and cutting them into bite-sized pieces.
6. When ready to serve, remove the tzatziki from the refrigerator and give it a good stir.
7. Arrange the vegetable crudites on a platter next to the tzatziki bowl.
8. Serve the tzatziki as a dip with the vegetable crudites on the side.

Turkish Cucumber, Mint, and Yogurt Dip (Cacik)

Servings: 4 | Preparation time: 45 minutes

Ingredients

- 2 medium-sized cucumbers (approximately 300g)
- 200g Greek yogurt
- 1 clove of garlic
- 1 tablespoon fresh mint leaves, finely chopped
- 1 tablespoon extra virgin olive oil
- 1 tablespoon lemon juice
- Salt and pepper, to taste

Nutrition facts per 100g:

Calories: 62
Total Fat: 5g
Saturated Fat: 1g
Total Carbohydrate: 3g
Dietary Fiber: 1g
Sugars: 2g
Protein: 2g

Preparation:

1. Start by preparing the cucumbers. Peel them, then cut them in half lengthwise. Use a spoon to scrape out the seeds, then grate the cucumbers using a box grater or a food processor.
2. Place the grated cucumber in a clean kitchen towel or a cheesecloth, then squeeze out as much liquid as possible. Transfer the cucumber to a mixing bowl.
3. Peel the garlic clove and finely mince it. Add it to the bowl with the cucumber.
4. Stir in the Greek yogurt, chopped mint leaves, olive oil, and lemon juice. Mix well to combine all the ingredients.
5. Season the dip with salt and pepper according to your taste preference. Give it a final stir.
6. Cover the bowl with cling film and refrigerate for at least 30 minutes to allow the flavours to blend together.
7. Before serving, give the dip a quick stir. If desired, garnish with a drizzle of olive oil and a sprinkle of additional chopped mint.
8. Serve the Turkish Cucumber, Mint, and Yogurt Dip with some pita bread, breadsticks, or vegetable sticks for dipping.

Moroccan Spiced Carrot Hummus

Servings: 4 | Preparation time: 10-12 minutes

Ingredients

- 400 grams of carrots, peeled and chopped
- 1 can (400 grams) of chickpeas, drained and rinsed
- 2 cloves of garlic, minced
- 2 tablespoons of olive oil
- Juice of 1 lemon
- 1 tablespoon of ground cumin
- 1 teaspoon of ground coriander
- Salt and pepper, to taste
- Fresh parsley, for garnish
- Toasted pita bread or vegetable crudites, for serving

Nutrition facts per 100g:

Calories: 103
Protein: 3.5g
Fat: 4.5g
Carbohydrates: 12.8g
Fiber: 3.5g
Sugars: 3.8g
Sodium: 230mg

Preparation:

1. In a medium-sized saucepan, bring water to a boil. Add in the chopped carrots and cook for about 10-12 minutes or until tender. Drain and set aside to cool slightly.
2. In a food processor, combine the cooked carrots, chickpeas, minced garlic, olive oil, lemon juice, cumin, coriander, salt, and pepper. Blitz until smooth and creamy, scraping down the sides of the processor as needed.
3. Taste and adjust the seasoning if necessary. If the hummus seems too thick, you can add a splash of water or more olive oil to reach your desired consistency.
4. Transfer the hummus to a serving bowl and drizzle with a little more olive oil. Sprinkle with fresh parsley for garnish.
5. Serve the Moroccan Spiced Carrot Hummus with toasted pita bread or vegetable crudites for a light and flavourful snack.

Sardinian Panada (Empanada-like Pastry)

Servings: 8 | Preparation time: 30 minutes

Ingredients

- 300g plain flour, plus extra for dusting
- 150g cold unsalted butter, cubed
- Pinch of salt
- 3 tablespoons ice-cold water
- 250g potatoes, peeled and cubed
- 150g canned tuna, drained
- 1 small onion, finely chopped
- 1 garlic clove, minced
- 1 tablespoon extra virgin olive oil
- Salt and pepper to taste
- 1 egg, beaten (for egg wash)

Nutrition facts per 100g:

Calories: 303
Total Fat: 19.4g
Saturated Fat: 11.7g
Trans Fat: 0g
Cholesterol: 74mg
Sodium: 193mg
Total Carbohydrate: 23.5g
Dietary Fiber: 1.2g
Sugars: 0.6g
Protein: 8.1g

Preparation:

1. In a large mixing bowl, combine the flour, butter, and salt. Use your fingertips to rub the butter into the flour until the mixture resembles breadcrumbs.
2. Gradually add the cold water, mixing until the dough comes together. Shape the dough into a ball, wrap it in cling film, and refrigerate for 30 minutes.
3. Meanwhile, boil the potatoes in salted water until tender. Drain and mash them in a bowl.
4. In a separate pan, sauté the onion and garlic in olive oil until softened. Add the canned tuna and mashed potatoes to the pan. Season with salt and pepper. Mix well and set aside to cool.
5. Preheat the oven to 180°C (350°F) and line a baking tray with parchment paper.
6. On a lightly floured surface, roll out the pastry to a thickness of about 3mm. Use a round cutter to cut out circles, approximately 10cm in diameter.
7. Place a spoonful of the tuna and potato filling in the center of each pastry circle. Fold the pastry over to form a half-moon shape and press the edges together to seal. Use a fork to crimp the edges.
8. Arrange the sardinian panadas on the prepared baking tray. Brush the tops with beaten egg for a golden finish.
9. Bake in the preheated oven for 25-30 minutes, or until the pastry is golden and crisp.
10. Allow the panadas to cool slightly before serving. They can be enjoyed warm or at room temperature. Serve as a light bite or a snack.

Spanish Almond-Stuffed Dates Wrapped in Bacon (Datiles con Tocino)

Servings: 12 | Preparation time: 30 minutes

Ingredients

- 12 Medjool dates, pitted
- 24 whole almonds
- 12 slices of streaky bacon
- Freshly ground black pepper, to taste
- Olive oil, for brushing

Nutrition facts per 100g:

Calories: 381
Total fat: 19.6g
Saturated fat: 5.5g
Cholesterol: 26mg
Sodium: 323mg
Total carbohydrates: 42.8g
Dietary fiber: 4.7g
Sugars: 30.2g
Protein: 9.4g

Preparation:

1. Preheat the oven to 190°C (375°F) and line a baking sheet with parchment paper.
2. Make a lengthwise slit in each date and remove the pit, creating a pocket.
3. Stuff each date with 2 whole almonds, pressing them gently into the pocket.
4. Season the stuffed dates with freshly ground black pepper.
5. Take a slice of streaky bacon and cut it in half widthwise.
6. Wrap each stuffed date with a half-slice of bacon, securing it with a toothpick if needed.
7. Place the bacon-wrapped dates on the prepared baking sheet.
8. Lightly brush the tops of the dates with a small amount of olive oil.
9. Bake in the preheated oven for 15-20 minutes, or until the bacon is crispy and golden brown.
10. Remove from the oven and let the dates cool slightly before serving.
11. Serve warm or at room temperature as a tasty Mediterranean-inspired appetizer or snack.

Turkish Cheese and Spinach Gozleme

Servings: 4 | Preparation time: 20 minutes

Ingredients

- 250g strong white bread flour
- ½ tsp salt
- 150ml warm water
- 1 tbsp olive oil
- 150g feta cheese, crumbled
- 250g fresh spinach, washed and roughly chopped
- 1 small red onion, finely chopped
- 2 cloves garlic, minced
- 1 tsp dried oregano
- Salt and pepper, to taste
- Olive oil, for frying

Nutrition facts per 100g:

Calories: 197
Fat: 8g
Saturated Fat: 4g
Cholesterol: 20mg
Sodium: 438mg
Carbohydrates: 23g
Fiber: 2g
Sugar: 1g
Protein: 8g

Preparation:

1. In a large bowl, combine the flour and salt. Make a well in the center and add the warm water and olive oil. Stir until a dough forms, then transfer to a floured surface and knead for about 5 minutes until smooth and elastic. Cover with a damp cloth and let it rest for 15 minutes.
2. In the meantime, prepare the filling. Heat a drizzle of olive oil in a pan over medium heat. Add the chopped onion and garlic, and sauté until softened. Add the spinach and cook until wilted. Season with oregano, salt, and pepper. Remove from heat and allow the mixture to cool slightly, then stir in the crumbled feta cheese.
3. Divide the dough into 4 equal portions. Roll each portion into a thin, rectangular shape on a floured surface. Spread the filling evenly on one half of each rectangle, leaving a small border around the edges.
4. Fold the dough over the filling and press the edges firmly to seal. You may need to lightly wet the edges with water to help seal them.
5. Heat a drizzle of olive oil in a large non-stick pan over medium heat. Cook each gozleme for about 4-5 minutes on each side until golden brown and crispy. Press down gently with a spatula while cooking to help melt the cheese and seal the edges.
6. Remove from the pan and cut each gozleme into smaller portions. Serve warm as a delicious light bite or snack.

Lebanese Lamb Kofta with Tahini Sauce

Servings: 4 | Preparation time: 10-15 minutes

Ingredients

- 500g minced lamb
- 1 small onion, finely chopped
- 2 cloves of garlic, minced
- 2 tablespoons finely chopped parsley
- 1 teaspoon ground cumin
- 1 teaspoon ground coriander
- 1/2 teaspoon ground cinnamon
- 1/2 teaspoon cayenne pepper (optional, for extra heat)
- Salt and pepper to taste
- Olive oil for grilling

Tahini Sauce:

- 4 tablespoons tahini
- Juice of 1 lemon
- 2 tablespoons water
- 1 clove of garlic, minced
- Salt to taste

Nutrition facts per 100g:

Calories: 245
Total Fat: 19.3g
Saturated Fat: 7.6g
Trans Fat: 0g
Cholesterol: 59mg
Sodium: 89mg
Total Carbohydrate: 1.4g
Dietary Fiber: 0.4g
Sugar: 0.2g
Protein: 17.4g

Preparation:

1. In a large bowl, combine minced lamb, chopped onion, minced garlic, parsley, ground cumin, ground coriander, ground cinnamon, cayenne pepper (if using), salt, and pepper.
2. Mix well using your hands, ensuring all the ingredients are fully incorporated.
3. Shape the mixture into small oval-shaped koftas, about 2 tablespoons of mixture for each kofta.
4. Preheat your grill or barbecue to medium-high heat.
5. Brush the koftas with olive oil to prevent sticking and place them on the grill.
6. Cook the koftas for about 8-10 minutes, turning occasionally, until they are browned and cooked through.
7. While the koftas are cooking, prepare the tahini sauce by combining tahini, lemon juice, water, minced garlic, and salt in a bowl. Whisk until smooth and creamy. Adjust the consistency by adding more water if needed.
8. Once cooked, remove the koftas from the grill and serve them hot with the tahini sauce on the side.
9. These Lebanese lamb koftas make a tasty and filling snack or light bite.

Italian Marinated Olives with Citrus and Fennel

Servings: 4 | Preparation time: 2 hours 15 minutes

Ingredients

- 200g mixed olives (green and black)
- Zest of 1 lemon
- Zest of 1 orange
- 1 tbsp fresh lemon juice
- 1 tbsp fresh orange juice
- 1 tbsp extra virgin olive oil
- 1 tsp fennel seeds
- 1 small garlic clove, minced
- Freshly ground black pepper, to taste

Nutrition facts per 100g:

Calories: 145
Total Fat: 13g
Saturated Fat: 2g
Trans Fat: 0g
Cholesterol: 0mg
Sodium: 790mg
Total Carbohydrate: 6g
Dietary Fiber: 3g
Total Sugars: 0g
Protein: 1g

Preparation:

1. In a mixing bowl, combine the lemon and orange zest, lemon juice, orange juice, olive oil, fennel seeds, minced garlic, and black pepper.
2. Drain the brine from the olives and add them to the marinade.
3. Toss the olives gently until they are well coated in the marinade.
4. Cover the bowl with plastic wrap and refrigerate for at least 2 hours, allowing the flavours to meld together.
5. Before serving, let the olives come to room temperature.
6. Serve the marinated olives in a bowl or small dish, with toothpicks or cocktail sticks for easy snacking.

Greek Spinach and Feta Cheese Triangles (Spanakopita)

Servings: 12 triangles | Preparation time: 35 minutes

Ingredients

- 250g fresh spinach, washed and chopped
- 250g feta cheese, crumbled
- 1 small onion, finely chopped
- 2 tablespoons fresh dill, chopped
- 2 tablespoons fresh parsley, chopped
- 2 tablespoons olive oil
- 6 sheets of filo pastry
- Salt and pepper, to taste
- Butter or cooking spray, for greasing

Nutrition facts per 100g:

Calories: 207
Total Fat: 13.5g
Saturated Fat: 7.3g
Cholesterol: 44mg
Sodium: 403mg
Total Carbohydrate: 14.8g
Dietary Fiber: 1g
Sugars: 1.3g
Protein: 8.9g

Preparation:

1. Preheat the oven to 180°C (350°F) and lightly grease a baking tray with butter or cooking spray.
2. In a large pan, heat the olive oil over medium heat. Add the chopped onion and cook until translucent.
3. Add the chopped spinach to the pan and cook until wilted. Remove from heat and let it cool slightly.
4. In a mixing bowl, combine the wilted spinach, crumbled feta cheese, chopped dill, and parsley. Season with salt and pepper to taste. Mix well until all ingredients are evenly distributed.
5. Lay one sheet of filo pastry on a clean, flat surface and lightly brush with melted butter or coat with cooking spray. Place another sheet of filo pastry on top and repeat the process until you have used three sheets in total.
6. Cut the layered filo pastry sheets into three equal strips lengthwise.
7. Place a spoonful of the spinach and feta mixture at one end of each strip. Fold the end over the mixture to form a triangle shape. Continue folding the triangle along the strip until you reach the end, ensuring a secure seal. Repeat this step for the remaining pastry and filling.
8. Arrange the triangles on the prepared baking tray and lightly brush the tops with melted butter or coat with cooking spray.
9. Bake in the preheated oven for 20-25 minutes, or until the triangles are golden brown and crispy.
10. Remove from the oven and let them cool slightly before serving. These Greek Spinach and Feta Cheese Triangles (Spanakopita) are delicious as a light bite or a snack.

Spanish Garlic Shrimp (Gambas al Ajillo)

Servings: 4 | Preparation time: 10 minutes

Ingredients

- 500g large raw prawns, peeled and deveined
- 4 tablespoons olive oil
- 4 garlic cloves, thinly sliced
- 1 teaspoon red chili flakes (adjust according to heat preference)
- 1 tablespoon fresh parsley, finely chopped
- 1 tablespoon lemon juice
- Salt, to taste

Nutrition facts per 100g:

Calories: 221 kcal
Protein: 20.6g
Carbohydrates: 2.3g
Fat: 14.7g
Fiber: 0.3g

Preparation:

1. In a large frying pan, heat the olive oil over medium heat.
2. Add the sliced garlic and red chili flakes to the pan and cook for about 2 minutes, stirring occasionally until the garlic turns golden and fragrant.
3. Increase the heat to high and add the prawns to the pan. Spread them out in a single layer to ensure even cooking.
4. Cook the prawns for 2-3 minutes on each side until they turn pink and opaque.
5. Sprinkle the prawns with salt and stir in the lemon juice and chopped parsley. Cook for an additional 1 minute to let the flavours meld together.
6. Remove the pan from the heat and let the shrimp rest for a minute before serving.
7. Transfer the Spanish garlic shrimp (gambas al ajillo) to a serving dish, spooning the garlic and chili oil over the top.
8. Serve hot as a light bite or snack, with crusty bread to mop up the delicious sauce.

Italian Bruschetta with Tomato and Basil

Servings: 4 | Preparation time: 15 minutes

Ingredients

- 4 slices of ciabatta bread (about 2 cm thick)
- 2 large ripe tomatoes
- 2 cloves of garlic
- Fresh basil leaves
- Extra virgin olive oil
- Salt and pepper to taste

Nutrition facts per 100g:

Calories: 219
Total Fat: 5.3g
Saturated Fat: 0.7g
Trans Fat: 0g
Cholesterol: 0mg
Sodium: 297mg
Total Carbohydrate: 36.5g
Dietary Fiber: 2.9g
Sugars: 2.8g
Protein: 6.2g

Preparation:

1. Preheat the grill to medium-high heat.
2. Toast the ciabatta slices on both sides until golden brown.
3. Peel the garlic cloves and cut them in half.
4. Rub the toasted bread with the cut side of the garlic to infuse the flavours.
5. Dice the tomatoes into small pieces and place them in a bowl.
6. Tear several basil leaves into small pieces and add them to the tomatoes.
7. Drizzle the tomato and basil mixture with olive oil and season with salt and pepper. Mix well.
8. Spoon the tomato and basil mixture generously over each slice of the garlic-rubbed ciabatta.
9. Add a final drizzle of olive oil over the topping.
10. Place the bruschetta under the grill for about 2-3 minutes, or until the tomatoes are slightly softened.
11. Remove from the grill and let it cool for a minute before serving.
12. Garnish with some fresh basil leaves and serve as a light bite or snack.

Turkish Sesame Seed-Crusted Simit Rolls

Servings: 12 rolls | Preparation time: 2 hours

Ingredients

- 300g plain flour
- 1 teaspoon salt
- 1 teaspoon sugar
- 7g dried yeast
- 200ml warm water
- 2 tablespoons olive oil
- 1 tablespoon sesame seeds
- 1 tablespoon poppy seeds

Nutrition facts per 100g:

Calories: 315
Total Fat: 7g
Saturated Fat: 1g
Sodium: 450mg
Total Carbohydrate: 54g
Sugars: 1g
Protein: 9g

Preparation:

1. In a large mixing bowl, combine the flour, salt, and sugar. In a separate small bowl, dissolve the yeast in warm water, and let it sit for about 5 minutes until it becomes frothy.
2. Slowly pour the yeast mixture and olive oil into the dry ingredients and mix until it forms a dough.
3. Transfer the dough onto a clean surface and knead it for about 5 minutes until it becomes smooth and elastic.
4. Place the dough back into the mixing bowl, cover it with a clean cloth, and let it rise in a warm place for about 1 hour until it doubles in size.
5. Preheat the oven to 200°C (180°C fan). Line a baking tray with parchment paper.
6. Punch down the risen dough and divide it into 12 equal portions. Roll each portion into a long rope shape, about 25cm in length.
7. Shape each rope into a circle, overlapping the ends slightly to seal them together, creating a round roll.
8. In a small bowl, mix together the sesame seeds and poppy seeds. Brush each roll with a little water and then dip the top of each roll into the seed mixture, ensuring they are evenly coated.
9. Place the seeded rolls onto the prepared baking tray and bake them in the preheated oven for 12-15 minutes or until they turn golden brown.
10. Remove the rolls from the oven and let them cool on a wire rack. Serve this delicious Turkish sesame seed-crusted simit rolls as a light snack or accompaniment to dips and spreads.

Greek Melitzanosalata (Aubergine Dip)

Servings: 4 | Preparation time: 1 hour

Ingredients

- 2 large aubergines (about 600g total)
- 3 tablespoons extra virgin olive oil
- 2 cloves garlic, minced
- 1 tablespoon lemon juice
- 2 tablespoons Greek yogurt
- 1 tablespoon fresh parsley, chopped
- Salt and pepper, to taste

Nutrition facts per 100g:

Calories: 90
Total Fat: 7g
Saturated Fat: 1g
Trans Fat: 0g
Total Carbohydrate: 6g
Dietary Fiber: 3g
Sugars: 2g
Protein: 2g

Preparation:

1. Preheat the oven to 200°C (180°C fan).
2. Prick the aubergines with a fork and place them on a baking tray.
3. Roast the aubergines for about 45 minutes or until the skin is charred and the flesh is soft.
4. Remove the aubergines from the oven and let them cool.
5. Once cooled, peel off the skin and discard it.
6. Chop the flesh into small pieces and place it in a colander to drain for about 10 minutes.
7. In a blender or food processor, combine the drained aubergine, minced garlic, lemon juice, and extra virgin olive oil. Blend until smooth.
8. Transfer the mixture to a bowl and stir in the Greek yogurt. Season with salt and pepper to taste.
9. Garnish with chopped parsley and a drizzle of extra virgin olive oil.
10. Serve the melitzanosalata with pita bread or vegetable sticks as a light bite or snack.

Moroccan Zaalouk (Aubergine and Tomato Dip)

Servings: 4 | Preparation time: 30 minutes

Ingredients

- 2 large aubergines (eggplants)
- 4 ripe tomatoes
- 1 red onion, finely chopped
- 4 cloves of garlic, minced
- 2 tablespoons of olive oil
- 1 teaspoon of ground cumin
- 1 teaspoon of ground coriander
- 1/2 teaspoon of smoked paprika
- 1/2 teaspoon of chili flakes (optional)
- Juice of 1 lemon
- Salt and pepper, to taste
- Fresh parsley or coriander leaves, for garnish

Nutrition facts per 100g:

Calories: 62
Fat: 3.7g
Saturated Fat: 0.5g
Trans Fat: 0g
Cholesterol: 0mg
Sodium: 4mg
Carbohydrates: 7.1g
Fiber: 3.2g
Sugar: 2.7g
Protein: 1.4g

Preparation:

1. Preheat the oven to 200°C (180°C fan). Prick the aubergines with a fork and place them on a baking tray. Roast in the oven for 25-30 minutes until the flesh is soft and the skin is charred. Remove from the oven and allow to cool slightly.
2. While the aubergines are roasting, prepare the tomatoes. Cut a small cross on the bottom of each tomato and blanch them in boiling water for about 30 seconds. Transfer the tomatoes to a bowl of ice water. Peel off the skin, remove the seeds, and finely chop the flesh.
3. In a large frying pan, heat the olive oil over medium heat. Add the chopped onion and minced garlic, cooking until soft and translucent.
4. Add the chopped tomatoes to the pan and cook for 5-7 minutes, until they start to break down and release their juices.
5. Meanwhile, peel off the charred skin from the roasted aubergines and roughly chop the flesh.
6. Add the chopped aubergines, ground cumin, ground coriander, smoked paprika, and chili flakes (if using) to the pan. Stir well to combine all the ingredients.
7. Reduce the heat to low and let the mixture simmer for about 10 minutes, stirring occasionally. The dip should thicken slightly.
8. Remove from heat and let the mixture cool for a few minutes. Stir in the lemon juice and season with salt and pepper to taste.
9. Transfer the dip to a serving bowl and garnish with fresh parsley or coriander leaves.
10. Serve the Moroccan Zaalouk with toasted pita bread, crackers, or fresh vegetables for a delicious and healthy snack.

Spanish Patatas Bravas

Servings: 4 | Preparation time: 35 minutes

Ingredients

- 700g potatoes, peeled and cut into small cubes
- 2 tablespoons olive oil
- 1 teaspoon paprika
- 1/2 teaspoon chili powder
- 1/2 teaspoon garlic powder
- 1/2 teaspoon salt
- 1/4 teaspoon black pepper

For the sauce:

- 2 tablespoons olive oil
- 1 onion, finely diced
- 2 garlic cloves, minced
- 1/2 teaspoon chili flakes
- 1 can (400g) chopped tomatoes
- 2 tablespoons tomato paste
- 1 tablespoon white wine vinegar
- 1 teaspoon smoked paprika
- 1/2 teaspoon sugar
- Salt and black pepper to taste

Nutrition facts per 100g:

Calories: 86
Total Fat: 3.7g
Saturated Fat: 0.5g
Trans Fat: 0g
Cholesterol: 0mg
Sodium: 172mg
Total Carbohydrate: 12.1g
Dietary Fiber: 1.8g
Sugars: 2.4g
Protein: 1.5g

Preparation:

1. Preheat the oven to 200°C (180°C fan). Place the potatoes in a large baking tray and drizzle with olive oil. Sprinkle with paprika, chili powder, garlic powder, salt, and black pepper. Toss well to coat the potatoes evenly.
2. Roast the potatoes in the preheated oven for 30-35 minutes, or until crisp and golden brown.
3. While the potatoes are cooking, prepare the sauce. Heat the olive oil in a saucepan over medium heat. Add the diced onion and cook until softened and lightly browned. Stir in the minced garlic and chili flakes, cooking for an additional minute.
4. Add the chopped tomatoes, tomato paste, white wine vinegar, smoked paprika, sugar, salt, and black pepper to the saucepan. Stir well to combine and bring the sauce to a simmer. Reduce the heat to low and let it simmer for 15 minutes, stirring occasionally.
5. Once the potatoes are ready, transfer them to a serving dish and pour the spicy tomato sauce over them. Serve immediately as a delicious light bite or snack.

Lebanese Zaatar Flatbread (Manakish)

Servings: 4 | Preparation time: 20-22 minutes

Ingredients

- 250 grams plain flour
- 5 grams instant yeast
- 1 teaspoon sugar
- 1 teaspoon salt
- 175 milliliters warm water
- 2 tablespoons olive oil, plus additional for brushing
- 2 tablespoons zaatar spice blend
- 1 tablespoon sesame seeds

Nutrition facts per 100g:

Calories: 280
Fat: 8g
Saturated Fat: 1g
Carbohydrates: 44g
Sugar: 1g
Protein: 7g
Fiber: 3g
Sodium: 250mg

Preparation:

1. In a large mixing bowl, combine the plain flour, yeast, sugar, and salt.
2. Make a well in the center of the dry ingredients and pour in the warm water and olive oil. Stir until a dough forms.
3. Transfer the dough onto a lightly floured surface and knead for about 5 minutes, until smooth and elastic.
4. Place the dough back into the mixing bowl, cover with a clean tea towel, and let it rise for 1 hour, or until doubled in size.
5. Preheat the oven to 220°C (200°C fan). Line a baking tray with parchment paper.
6. Punch down the dough and divide it into 4 equal portions. Roll each portion into a round disc, approximately 0.5cm thick.
7. Place the discs onto the prepared baking tray and brush the tops with olive oil.
8. Sprinkle the zaatar spice blend evenly over the flatbreads, then sprinkle sesame seeds on top.
9. Bake in the preheated oven for 10-12 minutes, or until the flatbreads are golden and crispy.
10. Remove from the oven and let them cool slightly before serving. Cut into wedges or squares and enjoy as a light bite or snack.

Greek Tyropita (Cheese Pie)

Servings: 12 servings | Preparation time: 1 hour

Ingredients

- 500g feta cheese
- 250g ricotta cheese
- 250g filo pastry sheets
- 3 eggs
- 1/4 cup olive oil
- 1/4 teaspoon black pepper
- 1/4 teaspoon dried oregano
- 1/4 teaspoon dried dill
- 1/4 teaspoon dried mint

Nutrition facts per 100g:

Calories: 305
Total Fat: 17g
Saturated Fat: 8g
Cholesterol: 86mg
Sodium: 628mg
Total Carbohydrate: 28g
Dietary Fiber: 1g
Sugars: 0g
Protein: 12g

Preparation:

1. Preheat your oven to 180°C (350°F) and lightly grease a baking dish.
2. In a large mixing bowl, crumble the feta cheese and add the ricotta cheese. Mix well until fully combined.
3. Beat the eggs in a separate bowl and then add them to the cheese mixture. Stir until the eggs are fully incorporated.
4. Add the black pepper, dried oregano, dried dill, and dried mint to the cheese mixture. Mix well to evenly distribute the herbs.
5. Unroll the filo pastry sheets onto a clean surface and cover them with a damp towel to prevent them from drying out.
6. Take one sheet of filo pastry and brush it lightly with olive oil. Place another sheet on top and brush it with olive oil as well. Repeat this process until you've used about half of the filo pastry sheets.
7. Spread the cheese mixture evenly over the oiled filo pastry layers in the baking dish.
8. Continue layering the remaining filo pastry sheets on top of the cheese mixture, brushing each sheet lightly with olive oil.
9. Brush the top layer of filo pastry with olive oil.
10. Using a sharp knife, score the top layer of filo pastry into small squares or triangles.
11. Bake in the preheated oven for about 45 minutes or until the pie is golden brown and crispy.
12. Remove from the oven and allow to cool slightly before serving.

Chapter 5: Refreshing Salads and Soups (15 Recipes)

Greek Horiatiki (Village Salad)

Servings: 4 | Preparation time: 20 minutes

Ingredients

- 3 medium ripe tomatoes (400g), cut into chunks
- 1 cucumber (200g), peeled and sliced
- 1 red onion (100g), thinly sliced
- 200g feta cheese, crumbled
- 100g Kalamata olives, pitted
- 1 green bell pepper (150g), sliced
- 2 tablespoons extra virgin olive oil
- 1 tablespoon red wine vinegar
- Salt and pepper, to taste
- Fresh oregano, for garnish

Nutrition facts per 100g:

Calories: 85
Total Fat: 6.7g
Saturated Fat: 3.5g
Cholesterol: 16mg
Sodium: 479mg
Total Carbohydrate: 3.6g
Dietary Fiber: 1g
Sugars: 2.5g
Protein: 3.3g

Preparation:

1. In a large bowl, combine the tomatoes, cucumber, red onion, feta cheese, Kalamata olives, and green bell pepper.
2. In a separate small bowl, whisk together the extra virgin olive oil and red wine vinegar. Season with salt and pepper.
3. Drizzle the dressing over the salad and gently toss until well coated.
4. Allow the salad to sit for about 10 minutes to let the flavours combine.
5. Transfer the salad to a serving dish and garnish with fresh oregano.
6. Serve the Greek Horiatiki salad as a refreshing appetizer or as a side dish with grilled meats or fish.

Lebanese Tabbouleh

Servings: 4 | Preparation time: 20 minutes

Ingredients

- 200 grams bulgur wheat
- 350 ml boiling water
- 2 large bunches of parsley (approximately 150 grams), finely chopped
- 150 grams cherry tomatoes, halved
- 1 small red onion, finely chopped
- 1 cucumber, diced
- Juice of 2 lemons
- 3 tablespoons extra virgin olive oil
- Salt and pepper to taste

Nutrition facts per 100g:

Calories: 101 kcal
Protein: 2.5g
Carbohydrates: 13.4g
Fat: 4.6g
Fiber: 2g

Preparation:

1. In a large bowl, place the bulgur wheat and pour the boiling water over it. Cover the bowl with a plate or cling film and let it sit for about 20 minutes or until the bulgur is cooked and has absorbed all the water.
2. Fluff the bulgur wheat with a fork and set it aside to cool down completely.
3. Meanwhile, prepare the rest of the ingredients. Chop the parsley finely, halve the cherry tomatoes, finely chop the red onion, and dice the cucumber.
4. In a separate small bowl, whisk together the lemon juice, olive oil, salt, and pepper to make a dressing.
5. Once the bulgur has cooled down, add the chopped parsley, cherry tomatoes, red onion, and cucumber to the bowl. Mix well to combine.
6. Pour the dressing over the salad and toss everything together until all the ingredients are evenly coated.
7. Let the tabbouleh sit for at least 10 minutes to allow the flavours to meld together.
8. Serve chilled as a refreshing salad or as a side dish with grilled chicken or fish.

Moroccan Lentil Soup (Harira)

Servings: 4 | Preparation time: 30 minutes

Ingredients

- 200g red lentils
- 1 onion, chopped
- 2 cloves of garlic, minced
- 1 carrot, diced
- 1 celery stalk, diced
- 1 can of chopped tomatoes
- 1 tablespoon tomato paste
- 1 teaspoon ground cumin
- 1 teaspoon ground coriander
- 1 teaspoon ground ginger
- 1/2 teaspoon ground cinnamon
- 1/2 teaspoon turmeric
- 1 liter vegetable stock
- 1 tablespoon olive oil
- Salt and pepper, to taste
- Fresh parsley, chopped (for garnish)
- Lemon wedges (for serving)

Nutrition facts per 100g:

Calories: 82 kcal
Protein: 4.7g
Fat: 1.4g
Carbohydrate: 12.8g
Fiber: 3.9g
Sugars: 2.4g
Sodium: 233mg

Preparation:

1. Heat the olive oil in a large soup pot over medium heat. Add the onion, garlic, carrot, and celery. Sauté until the vegetables are tender, about 5 minutes.
2. Stir in the tomato paste, cumin, coriander, ginger, cinnamon, and turmeric. Cook for another minute to release the flavours.
3. Add the red lentils, canned tomatoes, and vegetable stock to the pot. Bring to a boil, then reduce the heat to low and simmer for about 20 minutes, or until the lentils are cooked and tender.
4. Using an immersion blender or a regular blender, puree the soup until smooth. If using a regular blender, allow the soup to cool slightly before blending in batches.
5. Return the soup to the pot and season with salt and pepper to taste. Simmer for an additional 10 minutes to allow the flavours to meld together.
6. Ladle the Moroccan lentil soup into bowls and garnish with fresh parsley. Serve with lemon wedges on the side for squeezing over the soup.

EXCLUSIVE BONUS

40 Weight Loss Recipes

&

14 Days Meal Plan

Scan the QR-Code and receive
the FREE download:

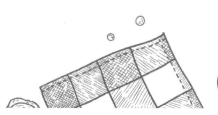

Greek White Bean Soup (Fasolada)

Servings: 4 | Preparation time: 2 hours

Ingredients

- 250g dried white beans
- 2 tablespoons olive oil
- 1 onion, chopped
- 2 carrots, diced
- 2 celery stalks, diced
- 3 garlic cloves, minced
- 1 bay leaf
- 400g canned chopped tomatoes
- 1 liter vegetable broth
- 1 tablespoon dried oregano
- Salt and pepper, to taste
- Fresh parsley, chopped for garnish

Nutrition facts per 100g:

Calories: 70 kcal
Total Fat: 1.9 g
Saturated Fat: 0.3 g
Total Carbohydrate: 10.3 g
Dietary Fiber: 3.4 g
Sugars: 2 g
Protein: 3.5 g

Preparation:

1. Soak the white beans in water overnight. Drain and rinse well.
2. In a large pot, heat the olive oil over medium heat. Add the onion, carrots, celery, and garlic. Cook for 5 minutes, or until the vegetables are softened.
3. Add the soaked white beans, bay leaf, canned chopped tomatoes, vegetable broth, dried oregano, salt, and pepper to the pot. Stir well to combine.
4. Bring the soup to a boil, then reduce the heat to low. Cover and simmer for 1 to 1.5 hours, or until the beans are tender.
5. Remove the bay leaf from the soup and discard. Use a blender or immersion blender to partially puree the soup, leaving some beans intact for texture.
6. Taste the soup and adjust the seasonings if needed. Add more salt, pepper, or dried oregano according to your preference.
7. Serve hot, garnished with freshly chopped parsley.

Italian Panzanella (Bread and Tomato Salad)

Servings: 4 | Preparation time: 35 minutes

Ingredients

- 400g ripe tomatoes, chopped into bite-sized pieces
- 200g stale rustic bread, cut into cubes
- 1 small red onion, thinly sliced
- 1 cucumber, deseeded and chopped
- 100g kalamata olives, pitted and halved
- 50g capers, rinsed and drained
- 10 fresh basil leaves, torn
- 3 tablespoons extra virgin olive oil
- 2 tablespoons red wine vinegar
- Salt and pepper, to taste

Nutrition facts per 100g:

Calories: 108
Total Fat: 5.3g
Saturated Fat: 0.8g
Total Carbohydrate: 13.9g
Dietary Fiber: 2.1g
Sugars: 3.5g
Protein: 2.3g

Preparation:

1. Preheat the oven to 180°C (350°F).
2. Spread the bread cubes on a baking tray and drizzle with 1 tablespoon of olive oil. Toss to coat. Bake in the oven for about 10 minutes or until crisp.
3. In a large salad bowl, combine the chopped tomatoes, red onion, cucumber, olives, capers, and torn basil leaves.
4. In a small bowl, whisk together the remaining olive oil, red wine vinegar, salt, and pepper to make the dressing.
5. Add the toasted bread cubes to the salad bowl and pour the dressing over. Toss everything together gently, ensuring the bread is well coated in the dressing and the flavours are evenly distributed.
6. Allow the panzanella salad to sit for 10-15 minutes, allowing the bread to soak up the dressing and the flavours to meld together.
7. Serve the Italian Panzanella as a refreshing and light lunch or as a side dish to accompany grilled meats or fish.

Spanish Gazpacho

Servings: 4 | Preparation time: 2 hours 20 minutes

Ingredients

- 1 kg ripe tomatoes, roughly chopped
- 1 cucumber, peeled and roughly chopped
- 1 red bell pepper, seeded and roughly chopped
- 1 small red onion, roughly chopped
- 2 garlic cloves, peeled
- 50 ml extra virgin olive oil
- 25 ml red wine vinegar
- 1 tsp sea salt
- 1/2 tsp black pepper
- 1/2 tsp smoked paprika
- A handful of fresh basil leaves, roughly torn

Nutrition facts per 100g:

Calories: 45
Fat: 3.5g
Saturated Fat: 0.5g
Carbohydrate: 3g
Fiber: 1g
Sugar: 2g
Protein: 1g

Preparation:

1. In a blender or food processor, combine the tomatoes, cucumber, red bell pepper, red onion, and garlic cloves. Blend until smooth.
2. Add the olive oil, red wine vinegar, sea salt, black pepper, and smoked paprika to the blender. Blend again until well combined.
3. Taste the gazpacho and adjust the seasonings if needed. If the mixture is too thick, you can add a splash of water and blend again.
4. Transfer the gazpacho to a large bowl or individual serving bowls.
5. Cover the bowl(s) with plastic wrap and refrigerate for at least 2 hours to allow the flavours to meld together.
6. Before serving, give the gazpacho a good stir and taste again to ensure it is seasoned to your liking.
7. Serve the Spanish gazpacho chilled, garnished with fresh basil leaves.

Cypriot Grain Salad with Pomegranate and Almonds

Servings: 4 | Preparation time: 30 minutes

Ingredients

- 200g bulgur wheat
- 300ml vegetable stock
- 1 cucumber, diced
- 200g cherry tomatoes, halved
- 1 red onion, finely chopped
- 100g pomegranate seeds
- 50g flaked almonds, toasted
- 1 small bunch fresh mint, chopped
- 1 small bunch fresh parsley, chopped
- Juice of 1 lemon
- 3 tablespoons extra virgin olive oil
- Salt and pepper, to taste

Nutrition facts per 100g:

Calories: 135
Total Fat: 7.1g
Saturated Fat: 0.7g
Trans Fat: 0g
Cholesterol: 0mg
Sodium: 54mg
Total Carbohydrate: 15.3g
Dietary Fiber: 5g
Sugars: 2.6g
Protein: 3.7g

Preparation:

1. In a saucepan, bring the vegetable stock to a boil. Add the bulgur wheat, reduce the heat to low, cover, and simmer for 15 minutes or until all the liquid has been absorbed. Remove from heat and let it cool.
2. In a large mixing bowl, combine the cooled bulgur wheat, cucumber, cherry tomatoes, red onion, pomegranate seeds, toasted almonds, mint, and parsley.
3. In a small bowl, whisk together the lemon juice, extra virgin olive oil, salt, and pepper to make the dressing.
4. Pour the dressing over the salad and toss gently to coat all the ingredients evenly.
5. Transfer the salad to a serving dish and refrigerate for at least 30 minutes to allow the flavours to meld.
6. Serve chilled as a refreshing salad on its own or as a side dish to grilled chicken or fish.

Moroccan Orange and Olive Salad

Servings: 4 | Preparation time: 40 minutes

Ingredients

- 3 large oranges
- 100g pitted green olives, sliced
- 1 small red onion, thinly sliced
- 2 tablespoons fresh parsley, chopped
- 2 tablespoons extra virgin olive oil
- 1 tablespoon lemon juice
- 1 teaspoon ground cumin
- Salt to taste
- Freshly ground black pepper to taste

Nutrition facts per 100g:

Calories: 97 kcal
Total Fat: 6.4g
Saturated Fat: 0.9g
Trans Fat: 0g
Cholesterol: 0mg
Sodium: 134mg
Total Carbohydrate: 10.6g
Dietary Fiber: 1.9g
Sugars: 7.8g
Protein: 1.2g

Preparation:

1. Peel the oranges, removing all the white pith, and slice them into rounds.
2. Place the orange slices in a serving bowl and scatter the sliced olives and red onion on top.
3. In a separate bowl, whisk together the olive oil, lemon juice, ground cumin, salt, and black pepper.
4. Drizzle the dressing over the salad and gently toss to combine all the ingredients.
5. Sprinkle the chopped parsley over the salad as a garnish.
6. Cover the bowl and refrigerate for at least 30 minutes to allow the flavours to meld.
7. Serve the Moroccan Orange and Olive Salad chilled as a refreshing appetizer or side dish.

Italian Minestrone Soup

Servings: 4 | Preparation time: 45 minutes

Ingredients

- 2 tablespoons olive oil
- 1 onion, diced
- 2 garlic cloves, minced
- 2 carrots, diced
- 2 celery stalks, diced
- 1 zucchini, diced
- 400g can chopped tomatoes
- 1.5 liters vegetable stock
- 200g canned cannellini beans, drained and rinsed
- 100g green beans, trimmed and chopped
- 100g small pasta (e.g. macaroni or shells)
- 1 teaspoon dried oregano
- Salt and pepper, to taste
- Parmesan cheese, grated (for serving)
- Fresh basil leaves, torn (for garnish)

Nutrition facts per 100g:

Calories: 47
Total Fat: 2g
Saturated Fat: 0.3g
Trans Fat: 0g
Cholesterol: 0mg
Sodium: 192mg
Total Carbohydrate: 6.6g
Dietary Fiber: 1.4g
Sugars: 2g
Protein: 1.4g

Preparation:

1. Heat the olive oil in a large pot over medium heat. Add the onions and garlic, and cook until softened.
2. Add the carrots, celery, and zucchini. Cook for a few more minutes until slightly tender.
3. Pour in the chopped tomatoes and vegetable stock. Bring to a boil, then reduce heat and let it simmer for 10 minutes.
4. Add the cannellini beans, green beans, and pasta. Simmer for an additional 10-15 minutes, or until the pasta is cooked.
5. Stir in the dried oregano and season with salt and pepper to taste.
6. Ladle the soup into bowls and top with grated Parmesan cheese.
7. Garnish with torn fresh basil leaves.
8. Serve hot and enjoy!

Greek Chickpea and Feta Salad

Servings: 4 | Preparation time: 45 minutes

Ingredients

- 200g canned chickpeas, drained and rinsed
- 150g cherry tomatoes, halved
- 1 cucumber, diced
- 100g feta cheese, crumbled
- 1 small red onion, thinly sliced
- 1 small bunch of fresh parsley, finely chopped
- 2 tablespoons extra virgin olive oil
- 1 tablespoon lemon juice
- Salt and pepper, to taste

Nutrition facts per 100g:

Calories: 107 kcal
Total fat: 6.5 g
Saturated fat: 1.8 g
Trans fat: 0 g
Total carbohydrates: 8.5 g
Dietary fiber: 2.4 g
Sugars: 2.3 g
Protein: 4.1 g

Preparation:

1. In a large mixing bowl, combine the chickpeas, cherry tomatoes, cucumber, feta cheese, red onion, and parsley.
2. In a small bowl, whisk together the olive oil, lemon juice, salt, and pepper to make the dressing.
3. Drizzle the dressing over the salad and gently toss until all the ingredients are well coated.
4. Allow the salad to marinate in the refrigerator for at least 30 minutes before serving to enhance the flavours.
5. Serve chilled as a refreshing salad on its own or as a side dish to complement your main course.

Turkish Red Lentil Soup (Mercimek Corbasi)

Servings: 4 | Preparation time: 35 minutes

Ingredients

- 200g red lentils
- 1 onion, finely chopped
- 2 carrots, finely diced
- 2 celery stalks, finely diced
- 4 cloves of garlic, minced
- 1 tbsp tomato paste
- 1 tsp ground cumin
- 1 tsp ground paprika
- 1 litre vegetable stock
- Juice of 1 lemon
- Salt and pepper, to taste
- Fresh parsley, chopped (for garnish)

Nutrition facts per 100g:

Calories: 86
Total Fat: 0.5g
Saturated Fat: 0.1g
Cholesterol: 0mg
Sodium: 307mg
Total Carbohydrate: 16.4g
Dietary Fiber: 4.9g
Sugars: 3g
Protein: 5.6g

Preparation:

1. Rinse the red lentils under cold running water until the water runs clear. Drain and set aside.
2. In a large pot, heat some olive oil and sauté the onion, carrots, celery, and garlic over medium heat until softened and slightly caramelized.
3. Stir in the tomato paste, ground cumin, and paprika. Cook for another minute to enhance the flavours.
4. Add the red lentils to the pot and pour in the vegetable stock. Bring to a boil, then reduce the heat and simmer uncovered for about 20-25 minutes, or until the lentils are tender.
5. Using an immersion blender, puree the soup until smooth and creamy. Alternatively, you can transfer it to a blender in batches, being careful when blending hot liquids.
6. Stir in the lemon juice and season with salt and pepper to taste.
7. Serve the Turkish Red Lentil Soup hot, garnished with freshly chopped parsley.

Italian Insalata Caprese

Servings: 4 | Preparation time: 20 minutes

Ingredients

- 4 large tomatoes
- 2 fresh mozzarella balls
- Handful of fresh basil leaves
- 2 tablespoons extra virgin olive oil
- 1 tablespoon balsamic vinegar
- Salt, to taste
- Pepper, to taste

Nutrition facts per 100g:

Calories: 157
Total Fat: 11g
Saturated Fat: 6g
Cholesterol: 33mg
Sodium: 318mg
Total Carbohydrate: 6g
Dietary Fiber: 1g
Sugars: 4g
Protein: 9g

Preparation:

1. Slice the tomatoes and mozzarella balls into equal-sized rounds.
2. Arrange the tomato and mozzarella slices alternately on a serving plate.
3. Tuck fresh basil leaves in between the tomato and mozzarella slices.
4. Drizzle extra virgin olive oil and balsamic vinegar over the salad.
5. Sprinkle salt and pepper to taste.
6. Allow the flavours to meld together for at least 10 minutes.
7. Serve the Insalata Caprese cold as an appetizer or side dish.

Greek Cucumber, Feta, and Olive Salad

Servings: 4 | Preparation time: 45 minutes

Ingredients

- 2 large cucumbers, peeled and diced
- 200g feta cheese, crumbled
- 200g cherry tomatoes, halved
- 100g kalamata olives, pitted and halved
- 1 small red onion, thinly sliced
- 2 tablespoons extra virgin olive oil
- 1 tablespoon red wine vinegar
- 1 tablespoon chopped fresh dill
- Salt, to taste
- Freshly ground black pepper, to taste

Nutrition facts per 100g:

Calories: 112
Total Fat: 8.8g
Saturated Fat: 4.8g
Cholesterol: 25mg
Sodium: 462mg
Total Carbohydrate: 4.6g
Dietary Fiber: 1.3g
Sugars: 2.1g
Protein: 4.6g

Preparation:

1. In a large mixing bowl, combine the diced cucumber, crumbled feta cheese, cherry tomatoes, olives, and sliced red onion.
2. In a small bowl, whisk together the extra virgin olive oil, red wine vinegar, chopped fresh dill, salt, and black pepper.
3. Pour the dressing over the salad and gently toss until all the ingredients are well coated.
4. Taste and adjust the seasoning if needed.
5. Cover the bowl with a cling film and refrigerate for at least 30 minutes to allow the flavours to meld together.
6. Once chilled, give the salad a final toss before serving.
7. Serve the refreshing Greek cucumber, feta, and olive salad as a side dish or as a light meal on its own.

French Nicoise Salad

Servings: 4 | Preparation time: 20 minutes

Ingredients

- 400g new potatoes, boiled and quartered
- 250g green beans, trimmed and blanched
- 200g cherry tomatoes, halved
- 200g canned tuna, drained
- 4 large eggs, hard-boiled and cut into quarters
- 100g black olives, pitted
- 100g anchovy fillets in oil, drained
- 1 small red onion, finely sliced
- 2 tablespoons capers
- 4 tablespoons extra virgin olive oil
- 2 tablespoons red wine vinegar
- Salt and pepper, to taste
- Fresh parsley, chopped (for garnish)

Nutrition facts per 100g:

Calories: 147
Total Fat: 10.1g
Saturated Fat: 1.9g
Trans Fat: 0g
Cholesterol: 47mg
Sodium: 391mg
Total Carbohydrate: 7.4g
Dietary Fiber: 1.6g
Sugars: 1.4g
Protein: 8.3g

Preparation:

1. In a large bowl, combine the potatoes, green beans, cherry tomatoes, tuna, eggs, black olives, anchovy fillets, red onion, and capers.
2. In a small bowl, whisk together the olive oil, red wine vinegar, salt, and pepper to make the dressing.
3. Drizzle the dressing over the salad and gently toss until well coated.
4. Divide the salad among four plates and garnish with fresh parsley.
5. Serve immediately and enjoy the refreshing flavours of this French Nicoise salad.

Turkish Shepherd's Salad (Çoban Salatası)

Servings: 4 | Preparation time: 45 minutes

Ingredients

- 2 medium cucumbers, diced
- 4 ripe tomatoes, diced
- 1 red onion, finely chopped
- 1 green bell pepper, diced
- 1/2 cup fresh parsley, finely chopped
- 1/4 cup fresh mint, finely chopped
- 1/4 cup extra virgin olive oil
- 2 tablespoons lemon juice
- Salt and pepper to taste

Nutrition facts per 100g:

Calories: 72
Total Fat: 5.5g
Saturated Fat: 0.8g
Cholesterol: 0mg
Sodium: 4mg
Total Carbohydrate: 5.8g
Dietary Fiber: 1.5g
Sugars: 3.1g
Protein: 1.1g

Preparation:

1. In a large mixing bowl, combine the diced cucumbers, tomatoes, red onion, green bell pepper, parsley, and mint.
2. Drizzle the extra virgin olive oil and lemon juice over the salad.
3. Season with salt and pepper according to your taste.
4. Toss all the ingredients together until well combined.
5. Cover the bowl with plastic wrap and refrigerate for at least 30 minutes to allow the flavours to meld.
6. Just before serving, give the salad a final toss and adjust the seasoning if needed.
7. Divide the Turkish Shepherd's Salad into individual bowls or plates and serve chilled.

Chapter 6: Delectable Seafood Delights (10 Recipes)

Sicilian Grilled Swordfish with Lemon and Herbs

Servings: 4 | Preparation time: 10 minutes

Ingredients

- 4 swordfish steaks (about 150g each)
- Zest of 1 lemon
- Juice of 1 lemon
- 2 cloves garlic, minced
- 2 tablespoons fresh parsley, chopped
- 2 tablespoons fresh thyme leaves
- 2 tablespoons extra virgin olive oil
- Salt and pepper, to taste

Nutrition facts per 100g:

Calories: 172 kcal
Total Fat: 8.3 g
Saturated Fat: 1.8 g
Carbohydrates: 1.1 g
Fiber: 0.3 g
Sugar: 0.3 g
Protein: 22.8 g

Preparation:

1. Preheat your grill to medium-high heat.
2. In a small bowl, combine the lemon zest, lemon juice, minced garlic, chopped parsley, thyme leaves, and extra virgin olive oil. Season with salt and pepper to taste.
3. Place the swordfish steaks in a shallow dish and pour the marinade over them, ensuring each steak is well coated. Allow them to marinate for at least 30 minutes, turning them once halfway through.
4. Remove the swordfish steaks from the marinade, shaking off any excess, and place them on the preheated grill. Reserve the marinade for basting later.
5. Grill the swordfish steaks for about 4-5 minutes per side or until cooked through and nicely charred. While grilling, baste the steaks with the reserved marinade occasionally to keep them moist and flavourful.
6. Once cooked, transfer the grilled swordfish to a platter and let them rest for a few minutes before serving.
7. Serve the Sicilian grilled swordfish steaks with lemon wedges on the side for an extra burst of freshness.

Spanish Seafood Paella

Servings: 4 | Preparation time: 20 minutes

Ingredients

- 300g paella rice
- 400g mixed seafood (such as prawns, mussels, squid)
- 1 onion, finely chopped
- 2 cloves of garlic, minced
- 1 red pepper, diced
- 1 tomato, diced
- 100g green beans, trimmed and halved
- 100g frozen peas
- 1 teaspoon smoked paprika
- 1 teaspoon saffron threads
- 1 liter seafood stock
- 2 tablespoons olive oil
- Fresh parsley, chopped, for garnish
- Lemon wedges, for serving

Nutrition facts per 100g:

Calories: 131 kcal
Protein: 7.4 g
Fat: 2.7 g
Carbohydrate: 19.3 g
Fiber: 1.2 g
Sugars: 1.3 g

Preparation:

1. In a large paella pan or wide skillet, heat the olive oil over medium heat. Add the onion and garlic and cook until soft and translucent.
2. Add the red pepper, tomato, green beans, and peas to the pan. Sauté for a few minutes until the vegetables are slightly softened.
3. Stir in the smoked paprika and saffron threads, ensuring all the ingredients are coated evenly.
4. Add the paella rice and spread it out in an even layer. Toast the rice for a minute or two, stirring occasionally.
5. Pour in the seafood stock and bring the mixture to a boil. Reduce the heat to low, cover the pan, and let it simmer for about 15 minutes until the rice is cooked and the liquid has been absorbed.
6. Meanwhile, cook the mixed seafood in a separate pan until cooked through. This should take around 4-5 minutes, depending on the size of the seafood.
7. Once the rice is cooked, arrange the cooked seafood on top of the rice in the pan. Cover and let it rest for a few minutes to allow the flavours to meld together.
8. Garnish with chopped parsley and serve hot with lemon wedges on the side.

Greek Octopus with Wine Sauce (Octapodi Krassato)

Servings: 4 | Preparation time: 60 minutes

Ingredients

- 1 kg octopus, cleaned and tentacles separated
- 500 ml dry white wine
- 2 onions, finely chopped
- 4 cloves garlic, minced
- 2 tomatoes, diced
- 1 bay leaf
- 2 tablespoons olive oil
- 2 tablespoons tomato paste
- 1 teaspoon dried oregano
- Salt and pepper, to taste
- Fresh parsley, for garnish

Nutrition facts per 100g:

Calories: 120 kcal
Fat: 3g
Cholesterol: 60mg
Sodium: 150mg
Carbohydrates: 5g
Fiber: 1g
Protein: 15g

Preparation:

1. In a large pot, bring the white wine to a boil. Add the octopus and reduce the heat to low. Simmer for 30 minutes until the octopus is tender. Drain and set aside.
2. In a separate pan, heat the olive oil over medium heat. Sauté the onions until translucent and then add the garlic. Cook for an additional minute until fragrant.
3. Stir in the diced tomatoes, tomato paste, bay leaf, dried oregano, salt, and pepper. Cook for 5 minutes to allow the flavours to meld.
4. Add the cooked octopus to the pan and toss to coat it with the tomato sauce. Simmer for another 15 minutes, stirring occasionally to ensure the octopus is evenly coated.
5. Remove from heat and transfer the octopus to a serving dish. Garnish with fresh parsley.
6. Serve the Greek Octopus with Wine Sauce (Octapodi Krassato) as a main course with crusty bread or over a bed of fluffy couscous.

Italian Seafood Risotto

Servings: 4 | Preparation time: 20-25 minutes

Ingredients

- 300g mixed seafood (such as prawns, mussels, and squid), cleaned
- 300g Arborio rice
- 1 small onion, finely chopped
- 2 cloves of garlic, minced
- 1 tablespoon olive oil
- 1 tablespoon butter
- 150ml dry white wine
- 800ml fish stock
- 1 teaspoon saffron threads
- 1 tablespoon chopped fresh parsley
- Salt and black pepper, to taste
- Lemon wedges, for serving

Nutrition facts per 100g:

Calories: 123 kcal
Total Fat: 3.2 g
Saturated Fat: 0.9 g
Total Carbohydrate: 15.5 g
Dietary Fiber: 0.3 g
Sugars: 0.6 g
Protein: 7.9 g

Preparation:

1. In a large pan, heat the olive oil and butter over medium heat. Add the chopped onion and minced garlic, and sauté until translucent and fragrant.
2. Add the Arborio rice to the pan and stir well, ensuring each grain is coated with the oil and butter mixture. Cook for a couple of minutes until the rice turns slightly translucent.
3. Pour in the white wine and cook until it evaporates, stirring continuously. Add the saffron threads to the fish stock and keep it simmering on a low heat.
4. Begin adding the fish stock to the rice, one ladleful at a time, stirring constantly. Allow the rice to absorb the liquid before adding more. Continue this process for about 15-18 minutes, or until the rice is al dente.
5. In a separate frying pan, heat a little olive oil and quickly cook the mixed seafood until just cooked through. Season with salt and black pepper to taste.
6. Once the rice is cooked, stir in the cooked seafood and chopped parsley, and gently mix until well combined.
7. Serve the Italian Seafood Risotto hot, garnished with extra parsley and lemon wedges on the side for squeezing over the dish.

Provençal Bouillabaisse with Rouille

Servings: 4 | Preparation time: 30 minutes

Ingredients

- 800g mixed seafood (e.g., prawns, mussels, squid, white fish)
- 2 tablespoons olive oil
- 1 onion, finely chopped
- 2 garlic cloves, minced
- 1 fennel bulb, thinly sliced
- 1 red bell pepper, thinly sliced
- 400g tin chopped tomatoes
- 500ml fish stock
- 125ml white wine
- 1 bay leaf
- 1 teaspoon dried thyme
- Salt and black pepper, to taste
- 4 slices of toasted baguette, for serving
- Rouille, for serving (see separate rouille recipe)

Nutrition facts per 100g:

Calories: 106 kcal
Total Fat: 3.8 g
Saturated Fat: 0.6 g
Trans Fat: 0 g
Total Carbohydrate: 5.4 g
Dietary Fiber: 1.3 g
Sugars: 2.9 g
Protein: 10.7 g

Preparation:

1. In a large pan, heat the olive oil over medium heat. Add the onion, garlic, fennel, and bell pepper. Sauté for 5 minutes until softened.
2. Add the tomatoes, fish stock, white wine, bay leaf, and thyme to the pan. Season with salt and black pepper. Bring to a boil, then reduce heat and simmer for 15-20 minutes to allow the flavours to meld.
3. Meanwhile, prepare the rouille using the separate recipe.
4. Add the mixed seafood to the pan and simmer for an additional 5-7 minutes until cooked through. Remove the bay leaf and discard.
5. Serve the bouillabaisse hot, ladled into bowls. Top each bowl with a slice of toasted baguette and a dollop of rouille.

Turkish Mussels Stuffed with Rice (Midye Dolma)

Servings: 4 | Preparation time: 25-30 minutes

Ingredients

- 500g fresh mussels
- 100g white rice
- 1 onion, finely chopped
- 2 tablespoons olive oil
- 1 tablespoon pine nuts
- 1 tablespoon currants
- 1 teaspoon ground cumin
- 1 teaspoon ground cinnamon
- 1 teaspoon dried mint
- Juice of 1 lemon
- Salt and pepper, to taste
- Fresh parsley, for garnish

Nutrition facts per 100g:

Calories: 133
Total Fat: 6.2g
Saturated Fat: 0.9g
Cholesterol: 23mg
Sodium: 179mg
Total Carbohydrate: 11.3g
Dietary Fiber: 1.4g
Sugars: 1.6g
Protein: 7.6g

Preparation:

1. Scrub the mussels under cold running water, removing any beards or impurities. Discard any mussels that are cracked or fail to close when tapped.
2. Cook the rice according to package instructions until it is al dente. Drain and set aside.
3. Heat the olive oil in a large frying pan over medium heat. Add the chopped onion and cook until soft and translucent, about 5 minutes.
4. Add the pine nuts, currants, cumin, cinnamon, and dried mint to the pan. Stir well and cook for an additional 2 minutes.
5. Next, add the cooked rice to the pan, stirring to combine all the flavours. Season with salt and pepper to taste. Remove from heat and let the stuffing mixture cool slightly.
6. Preheat the oven to 180°C/350°F.
7. On each mussel, gently pry open the shell and remove the flesh, leaving the hinge attached. Rinse the shells thoroughly.
8. Stuff each mussel shell with a spoonful of the rice mixture, pressing it in gently to ensure it fills the shell. Place the filled shells in a baking dish.
9. Drizzle the lemon juice over the stuffed mussels and bake in the preheated oven for 15-20 minutes, or until the mussels are cooked through and the rice is golden brown.
10. Once cooked, remove from the oven and let them cool slightly. Garnish with fresh parsley before serving.

Italian Linguine alle Vongole (Clam Pasta)

Servings: 4 | Preparation time: 20 minutes

Ingredients

- 400g linguine pasta
- 1kg fresh clams, scrubbed and rinsed
- 4 tablespoons extra virgin olive oil
- 4 garlic cloves, minced
- 1 red chili, sliced (optional for some heat)
- 200ml dry white wine
- 1 small bunch of fresh parsley, finely chopped
- Salt and black pepper to taste

Nutrition facts per 100g:

Calories: 167
Total Fat: 5.4g
Saturated Fat: 0.8g
Trans Fat: 0g
Cholesterol: 20mg
Sodium: 113mg
Total Carbohydrate: 20g
Dietary Fiber: 1.2g
Sugars: 0.7g
Protein: 7.4g

Preparation:

1. Bring a large pot of salted water to boil and cook the linguine according to the package instructions until al dente. Drain and set aside.
2. In a large skillet, heat the olive oil over medium heat. Add the minced garlic and sliced chili (if using) and sauté for about a minute until fragrant.
3. Add the clams to the skillet and pour in the white wine. Increase the heat to medium-high, cover the skillet, and let the clams cook for about 5 minutes or until they open. Discard any clams that do not open.
4. Once the clams have opened, remove them from the skillet and set aside. Continue simmering the liquid in the skillet for a few more minutes to reduce slightly.
5. Add the cooked linguine to the skillet and toss it in the flavourful liquid, ensuring the pasta is well-coated. Cook for an additional minute until the pasta absorbs some of the sauce.
6. Return the clams to the skillet along with the chopped parsley. Give it all a good mix.
7. Season with salt and black pepper to taste.

Moroccan Grilled Sardines

Servings: 4 | Preparation time: 25 minutes

Ingredients

- 12 fresh sardines, gutted and scaled
- 3 tablespoons olive oil
- 3 cloves garlic, minced
- 1 teaspoon ground cumin
- 1 teaspoon paprika
- 1 teaspoon ground coriander
- 1 teaspoon ground ginger
- 1 teaspoon salt
- Juice of 1 lemon
- Fresh parsley, chopped (for garnish)
- Lemon wedges (for serving)

Nutrition facts per 100g:

Calories: 218
Total Fat: 16g
Saturated Fat: 3g
Cholesterol: 66mg
Sodium: 371mg
Total Carbohydrate: 1g
Fiber: 0g
Sugars: 0g
Protein: 18g

Preparation:

1. Preheat the grill to medium-high heat.
2. In a small bowl, mix together the olive oil, minced garlic, cumin, paprika, coriander, ginger, salt, and lemon juice to create a marinade.
3. Place the sardines in a shallow dish and coat them evenly with the marinade. Let them marinate for at least 15 minutes.
4. Place the marinated sardines on the preheated grill and cook for approximately 3-4 minutes on each side or until they are cooked through and slightly charred.
5. Remove the grilled sardines from the grill and transfer them to a serving platter.
6. Garnish the sardines with freshly chopped parsley.
7. Serve the Moroccan Grilled Sardines hot with lemon wedges on the side.

Greek Baked Shrimp with Feta (Garides Saganaki)

Servings: 4 | Preparation time: 30-35 minutes

Ingredients

- 500g large raw shrimp, peeled and deveined
- 1 tablespoon olive oil
- 1 small onion, finely chopped
- 2 garlic cloves, minced
- 1 can (400g) diced tomatoes
- 1/4 cup dry white wine
- 1 teaspoon dried oregano
- 1/2 teaspoon dried thyme
- Salt and black pepper, to taste
- 100g feta cheese, crumbled
- Fresh parsley, chopped (for garnish)

Nutrition facts per 100g:

Calories: 136
Fat: 5.8g
Saturated Fat: 2.9g
Cholesterol: 175mg
Sodium: 336mg
Carbohydrate: 5.1g
Fiber: 1g
Sugar: 2g
Protein: 17.2g

Preparation:

1. Preheat the oven to 200°C (180°C fan).
2. In a large frying pan, heat the olive oil over medium heat. Add the onion and garlic, and sauté until softened, about 5 minutes.
3. Add the diced tomatoes, white wine, dried oregano, dried thyme, salt, and black pepper to the pan. Stir to combine and bring to a simmer. Cook for 10 minutes, until the sauce thickens slightly.
4. Place the cleaned shrimp in a baking dish and pour the tomato sauce over them, making sure they are well coated.
5. Sprinkle the crumbled feta cheese evenly over the shrimp.
6. Bake in the preheated oven for 15-20 minutes, until the shrimp are pink and cooked through, and the cheese is golden and bubbly.
7. Garnish with fresh parsley before serving.
8. Serve the Greek Baked Shrimp with Feta hot, alongside crusty bread or over a bed of cooked rice or orzo.

Italian Seafood Cioppino Stew

Servings: 4 | Preparation time: 20 minutes

Ingredients

- 500g mixed seafood (such as prawns, mussels, clams, and white fish)
- 1 onion, finely chopped
- 2 garlic cloves, minced
- 1 red bell pepper, sliced
- 1 carrot, sliced
- 400g tin of chopped tomatoes
- 250ml fish stock
- 125ml white wine
- 2 tablespoons olive oil
- 1 teaspoon dried oregano
- 1 teaspoon dried basil
- Salt and pepper, to taste
- Fresh parsley, chopped (for garnish)

Nutrition facts per 100g:

Calories: 71
Total Fat: 2.2g
Saturated Fat: 0.4g
Trans Fat: 0g
Cholesterol: 48mg
Sodium: 193mg
Total Carbohydrate: 3.2g
Dietary Fiber: 0.8g
Sugars: 1.4g
Protein: 9.2g

Preparation:

1. In a large pot, heat the olive oil over medium heat. Add the onion, garlic, and bell pepper. Sauté for 5 minutes until softened.
2. Add the carrot, oregano, and basil to the pot. Cook for another 3 minutes.
3. Pour in the white wine and allow it to simmer for 2 minutes until slightly reduced.
4. Add the chopped tomatoes and fish stock to the pot. Season with salt and pepper. Bring to a gentle simmer.
5. Reduce the heat to low. Cover the pot and let the stew simmer for 15 minutes to develop the flavours.
6. Meanwhile, clean the seafood well, removing any shells or beards from the mussels and clams.
7. After 15 minutes, add the seafood to the pot, stirring gently to combine. Cook for an additional 5 minutes until the seafood is tender and cooked through.
8. Taste and adjust seasoning if required.
9. Serve the Italian seafood cioppino stew in bowls, garnished with fresh parsley.

Chapter 7: Indulgent Vegan and Vegetarian Dishes (10 Recipes)

Greek Stuffed Bell Peppers with Rice (Yemista)

Servings: 4-6 servings | Preparation time: 1 hour 20 minutes

Ingredients

- 6 large bell peppers (any color)
- 200g long-grain rice
- 1 small onion, finely chopped
- 2 cloves garlic, minced
- 1 medium carrot, finely diced
- 1 small zucchini, finely diced
- 4 tomatoes, grated
- 1/4 cup fresh parsley, chopped
- 2 tablespoons fresh dill, chopped
- 2 tablespoons extra virgin olive oil, plus extra for drizzling
- Salt and pepper to taste

Nutrition facts per 100g:

Calories: 81
Protein: 2g
Fat: 3g
Saturated fat: 0.4g
Carbohydrates: 12g
Fiber: 2g
Sugar: 3g
Sodium: 85mg
Potassium: 235mg

Preparation:

1. Preheat the oven to 180°C.
2. Cut off the tops of the bell peppers and remove the seeds and membranes. Set aside.
3. In a large bowl, combine the rice, onion, garlic, carrot, zucchini, tomatoes, parsley, dill, olive oil, salt, and pepper. Mix well until all ingredients are evenly distributed.
4. Stuff the bell peppers with the rice mixture, packing it tightly. Place the stuffed peppers in a baking dish.
5. Drizzle each stuffed pepper with a little olive oil, then cover the dish with aluminum foil.
6. Bake in the preheated oven for 45 minutes.
7. After 45 minutes, remove the foil and continue baking for another 15 minutes, or until the peppers are tender and slightly charred on top.
8. Remove from the oven and let the stuffed peppers cool for a few minutes before serving.
9. Serve the Greek stuffed bell peppers as a main dish or as a side alongside a fresh salad.

Italian Vegan Lasagna with Cashew Ricotta

Servings: 6 | Preparation time: 45 minutes

Ingredients

Lasagna Sheets:

- 300g lasagna sheets

Vegetable Filling:

- 2 tablespoons olive oil
- 1 red onion, diced
- 2 garlic cloves, minced
- 1 red bell pepper, diced
- 1 zucchini, diced
- 200g mushrooms, sliced
- 400g can chopped tomatoes
- 2 tablespoons tomato paste
- 1 teaspoon dried oregano
- 1 teaspoon dried basil
- Salt and pepper, to taste

Cashew Ricotta:

- 200g raw cashews, soaked overnight and drained
- 3 tablespoons nutritional yeast
- 1 tablespoon lemon juice
- 2 garlic cloves, minced
- 150ml water
- Salt, to taste

Nutrition facts per 100g:

Calories: 136
Total Fat: 6.2g
Saturated Fat: 1.1g
Cholesterol: 0mg
Sodium: 119mg
Total Carbohydrate: 16.5g
Dietary Fiber: 2.8g
Sugars: 3.5g
Protein: 4.7g

Preparation:

1. Preheat the oven to 180°C (350°F) and lightly grease a baking dish.
2. In a large pan, heat the olive oil over medium heat. Add the onion and garlic, and sauté until softened.
3. Add the diced red bell pepper, zucchini, and mushrooms to the pan. Cook for around 5 minutes or until the vegetables are tender.
4. Stir in the chopped tomatoes, tomato paste, dried oregano, dried basil, salt, and pepper. Allow the mixture to simmer for about 10 minutes.
5. Meanwhile, prepare the cashew ricotta by blending the soaked cashews, nutritional yeast, lemon juice, minced garlic, water, and salt in a high-speed blender until smooth and creamy.
6. In the greased baking dish, spread a small amount of the vegetable filling on the bottom. Layer with lasagna sheets, cashew ricotta, and vegetable filling. Repeat until all the ingredients are used, finishing with a layer of lasagna sheets on top.
7. Cover the baking dish with foil and bake for 30 minutes. Remove the foil and bake for an additional 10 minutes or until the lasagna sheets are cooked through and the top is golden.
8. Allow the lasagna to cool for a few minutes before serving. Serve warm with a side salad, if desired.

Turkish Eggplant Kebab (Patlıcan Kebabı)

Servings: 4 | Preparation time: 25 minutes

Ingredients

- 4 medium-sized eggplants (500g)
- 2 medium-sized tomatoes
- 1 small red onion
- 2 cloves of garlic
- 2 tablespoons olive oil
- 2 tablespoons lemon juice
- 1 teaspoon oregano
- 1 teaspoon paprika
- Salt and pepper to taste
- Fresh parsley for garnish

Nutrition facts per 100g:

Calories: 88
Total Fat: 4g
Saturated Fat: <1g
Trans Fat: 0g
Cholesterol: 0mg
Sodium: 67mg
Total Carbohydrate: 12g
Dietary Fiber: 6g
Sugars: 6g
Protein: 2g

Preparation:

1. Preheat the grill to medium-high heat.
2. Slice the eggplants lengthwise into 1 cm thick strips. Place them in a colander and sprinkle with salt. Let them sit for 15 minutes to remove excess moisture.
3. Rinse the eggplant slices under cold water and pat dry with a paper towel.
4. Slice the tomatoes and red onion into thin rounds. Mince the garlic cloves.
5. In a bowl, combine the olive oil, lemon juice, oregano, paprika, minced garlic, salt, and pepper. Whisk the mixture until well combined.
6. Brush the eggplant slices on both sides with the olive oil mixture.
7. Thread the eggplant slices onto skewers alternately with tomato and red onion slices.
8. Place the kebabs on the preheated grill and cook for 3-4 minutes on each side until tender and lightly charred.
9. Remove the kebabs from the grill and sprinkle with fresh parsley.
10. Serve the Turkish eggplant kebabs hot with a side of whole grain pita bread or tabbouleh salad for a complete Mediterranean meal.

Lebanese Stuffed Zucchini (Kousa Mahshi)

Servings: 4 | Preparation time: 55-60 minutes

Ingredients

- 4 medium zucchini
- 200g basmati rice
- 1 onion, finely chopped
- 2 cloves of garlic, minced
- 200g canned chickpeas, drained and rinsed
- 2 tomatoes, diced
- 1 tbsp tomato paste
- 2 tbsp olive oil
- 1 tsp ground cumin
- 1 tsp ground coriander
- 1/2 tsp ground cinnamon
- 1/4 tsp ground allspice
- Salt and pepper, to taste
- Fresh parsley, for garnish

Nutrition facts per 100g:

Calories: 111
Protein: 3.4g
Fat: 3.3g (Saturated fat: 0.5g)
Carbohydrates: 18.3g (Sugar: 2.4g)
Fiber: 1.1g
Sodium: 73mg

Preparation:

1. Preheat the oven to 180°C (350°F). Leave the zucchini whole but trim off the tops and using a vegetable corer or sharp knife, carefully remove the insides of the zucchini, creating a hollow cavity.
2. Rinse the zucchini and set aside. Cook the basmati rice according to package instructions until it's almost cooked but still has a slight bite.
3. Heat the olive oil in a large pan over medium heat. Add the chopped onion and garlic, and sauté until translucent and fragrant.
4. Stir in the tomato paste, diced tomatoes, chickpeas, ground cumin, coriander, cinnamon, allspice, salt, and pepper. Cook for another 5 minutes, allowing the flavours to blend.
5. Remove the pan from heat and mix in the cooked basmati rice. Taste and adjust the seasoning if needed.
6. Stuff the hollow zucchini with the rice mixture, making sure to pack it in tightly. Place the stuffed zucchini in a large baking dish.
7. Pour about 250ml (1 cup) of water into the baking dish, ensuring the water is covering the bottom but not touching the stuffed zucchini. This will help to steam the zucchini while baking.
8. Cover the baking dish with aluminum foil and bake in the preheated oven for 30-35 minutes or until the zucchini is tender.
9. Remove the foil and continue baking for another 10 minutes or until the tops become golden brown.
10. Once cooked, remove from the oven and let the Lebanese stuffed zucchini cool slightly before serving. Garnish with fresh parsley and enjoy!

Greek Lentil and Spinach Soup with Lemon (Fakes Soupa)

Servings: 4 | Preparation time: 30-40 minutes

Ingredients

- 250 grams dried green lentils
- 2 tablespoons olive oil
- 1 large onion, finely chopped
- 3 cloves garlic, minced
- 1 carrot, diced
- 1 celery stalk, diced
- 1 bay leaf
- 1 teaspoon dried oregano
- 1 teaspoon dried thyme
- 250 grams fresh spinach, roughly chopped
- Juice of 1 lemon
- Salt and pepper, to taste

Nutrition facts per 100g:

Calories: 103
Total Fat: 3g
Saturated Fat: 0.4g
Trans Fat: 0g
Cholesterol: 0mg
Sodium: 196mg
Total Carbohydrate: 15g
Dietary Fiber: 6g
Sugars: 2g
Protein: 6g

Preparation:

1. Rinse the lentils under cold water and drain well.
2. In a large pot, heat the olive oil over medium heat. Add the onion, garlic, carrot, and celery. Sauté until the onion becomes translucent.
3. Add the lentils, bay leaf, dried oregano, dried thyme, and enough water to cover everything by about 2 cm. Bring to a boil, then reduce the heat and let simmer for about 30-40 minutes or until the lentils are tender.
4. Once the lentils are cooked, stir in the chopped spinach and let it wilt for a few minutes.
5. Remove the bay leaf and season the soup with lemon juice, salt, and pepper to taste.
6. Serve the Greek lentil and spinach soup hot, garnished with some freshly chopped parsley if desired.

Italian Vegan Osso Buco with Gremolata

Servings: 4 | Preparation time: 1 hour 15 minutes

Ingredients

- 4 vegan veal cutlets (seitan or tofu can be used as a substitute), about 200g each
- 2 tablespoons olive oil
- 1 medium onion, diced
- 2 cloves of garlic, minced
- 2 medium carrots, diced
- 2 celery stalks, diced
- 200ml vegetable broth
- 400g can of chopped tomatoes
- 200ml red wine
- 1 sprig of fresh rosemary
- 2 bay leaves
- Salt and pepper, to taste

For the Gremolata:

- Zest of 1 lemon
- 2 tablespoons fresh parsley, finely chopped
- 1 clove of garlic, minced

Nutrition facts per 100g:

Calories: 150
Total Fat: 8g
Saturated Fat: 1g
Cholesterol: 0mg
Sodium: 200mg
Total Carbohydrate: 10g
Dietary Fiber: 2g
Sugar: 4g
Protein: 10g

Preparation:

1. Start by heating the olive oil in a large saucepan or Dutch oven over medium heat. Add the diced onion and minced garlic. Sauté until the onion becomes translucent.
2. Add the diced carrots and celery to the pan and cook for another 2 minutes, stirring occasionally.
3. Push the vegetables to the sides of the pan to create a space in the center. Place the vegan veal cutlets in the center and sear them for 2-3 minutes on each side until browned.
4. Pour in the vegetable broth, chopped tomatoes, and red wine. Add the fresh rosemary, bay leaves, and season with salt and pepper to taste. Bring the mixture to a simmer, then reduce the heat to low. Cover the pan and let it cook for about 1 hour, or until the vegan veal is tender.
5. While the osso buco simmers, prepare the gremolata. In a small bowl, combine the lemon zest, chopped parsley, and minced garlic. Mix well and set aside.
6. Once the osso buco is cooked, remove the vegan veal cutlets from the pan and set them aside. Turn the heat up to medium-high and let the sauce reduce for about 5 minutes, stirring occasionally.
7. To serve, place each vegan veal cutlet on a plate, spoon the thickened sauce over the top, and sprinkle with the gremolata. Serve with a side of creamy polenta or mashed potatoes, and enjoy this indulgent vegan Italian dish!

Moroccan Vegetable Tagine with Preserved Lemon

Servings: 4 | Preparation time: 35 minutes

Ingredients

- 2 tablespoons olive oil
- 1 onion, sliced
- 2 garlic cloves, minced
- 2 teaspoons ground cumin
- 2 teaspoons ground coriander
- 1 teaspoon ground turmeric
- 1 teaspoon ground cinnamon
- 1 teaspoon paprika
- 1 teaspoon dried chili flakes (optional)
- 2 carrots, peeled and sliced
- 2 bell peppers, deseeded and sliced
- 1 small butternut squash, peeled and diced
- 1 can (400g) chickpeas, drained and rinsed
- 1 can (400g) chopped tomatoes
- 2 cups vegetable broth
- 1 preserved lemon, flesh removed, rind thinly sliced
- Handful of fresh cilantro, chopped
- Salt and pepper, to taste
- Couscous or rice, to serve

Nutrition facts per 100g:

Calories: 70
Total Fat: 3g
Saturated Fat: 0g
Trans Fat: 0g
Cholesterol: 0mg
Sodium: 100mg
Total Carbohydrate: 10g
Dietary Fiber: 2g
Sugars: 3g
Protein: 2g

Preparation:

1. Heat the olive oil in a large, heavy-bottomed pot over medium heat. Add the onion and garlic, and cook until softened and fragrant, around 5 minutes.
2. Add the cumin, coriander, turmeric, cinnamon, paprika, and chili flakes to the pot. Stir well to coat the onions and garlic with the spices.
3. Add the carrots, bell peppers, butternut squash, chickpeas, chopped tomatoes, and vegetable broth to the pot. Stir to combine.
4. Bring the mixture to a boil, then reduce the heat and simmer for 20-25 minutes, or until the vegetables are tender.
5. Stir in the preserved lemon slices and chopped cilantro. Season with salt and pepper to taste.
6. Serve the vegetable tagine over couscous or rice. Garnish with additional cilantro, if desired.

Sicilian Caponata (Eggplant Stew)

Servings: 4 | Preparation time: 40-45 minutes

Ingredients

- 2 medium-sized eggplants (about 500g)
- 2 tablespoons extra virgin olive oil
- 1 small red onion, finely chopped
- 2 cloves of garlic, minced
- 1 red bell pepper, diced
- 1 yellow bell pepper, diced
- 1 celery stalk, finely chopped
- 400g tin of chopped tomatoes
- 2 tablespoons tomato paste
- 3 tablespoons red wine vinegar
- 2 tablespoons capers, drained
- 2 tablespoons green olives, pitted and sliced
- 2 tablespoons raisins
- 1 tablespoon sugar
- Salt and pepper, to taste
- Fresh basil leaves, torn, for garnish

Nutrition facts per 100g:

Calories: 85
Total Fat: 3g
Saturated Fat: 0.4g
Cholesterol: 0mg
Sodium: 249mg
Total Carbohydrate: 14g
Dietary Fiber: 4g
Total Sugars: 9g
Protein: 2g

Preparation:

1. Start by preparing the eggplants. Cut them into small cubes, sprinkle some salt over them, and let them sit in a colander for about 30 minutes. This will help remove any excess bitterness. Rinse and pat dry with a clean tea towel.
2. Place a large pot over medium heat and add the olive oil. Once heated, add the onion and garlic, and sauté until softened.
3. Add the bell peppers and celery to the pot, and cook for a few minutes until they start to soften.
4. Add the eggplant cubes to the pot and cook for about 10 minutes until they become tender.
5. Stir in the chopped tomatoes, tomato paste, red wine vinegar, capers, olives, raisins, sugar, salt, and pepper. Mix well to combine all the flavours.
6. Reduce the heat to low, cover the pot, and let the caponata simmer for about 20-25 minutes, stirring occasionally.
7. Once the caponata has thickened and the flavours have melded together, remove it from the heat.
8. Serve the Sicilian caponata warm or at room temperature, garnished with fresh basil leaves.

Greek Gigantes Plaki (Baked Giant Beans)

Servings: 4 | Preparation time: 1 ½ to 2 hours

Ingredients

- 250g dried giant beans (lima beans)
- 1 onion, finely chopped
- 3 garlic cloves, minced
- 1 carrot, peeled and diced
- 1 celery stalk, diced
- 400g can chopped tomatoes
- 2 tablespoons tomato paste
- 1 teaspoon dried oregano
- 1 teaspoon dried thyme
- 1 teaspoon smoked paprika
- 1 tablespoon olive oil
- Salt and pepper, to taste
- Fresh parsley, chopped (for garnish)

Nutrition facts per 100g:

Calories: 112
Protein: 6g
Carbohydrates: 19g
Fat: 1g
Fiber: 6g

Preparation:

1. Soak the dried giant beans in cold water overnight. Drain and rinse before use.
2. Preheat the oven to 180°C (350°F).
3. In a large saucepan, heat the olive oil over medium heat. Add the chopped onion and cook until softened.
4. Add the minced garlic, carrot, and celery to the pan. Sauté for another 5 minutes until fragrant and slightly tender.
5. Stir in the tomato paste, dried oregano, dried thyme, and smoked paprika. Cook for 1-2 minutes to allow the flavours to meld together.
6. Add the drained and rinsed giant beans to the pot. Pour in the chopped tomatoes and season with salt and pepper. Stir well to combine.
7. Transfer the mixture to a baking dish and cover tightly with foil. Bake in the preheated oven for 1 ½ to 2 hours until the beans are tender and the sauce has thickened.
8. Remove the foil and continue to bake for an additional 10-15 minutes for a slightly crispy top.
9. Once cooked, remove from the oven and let it rest for 5 minutes before serving.
10. Garnish with freshly chopped parsley and serve warm.

Spanish Vegan Paella with Artichokes and Olives

Servings: 4 | Preparation time: 40 minutes

Ingredients

- 250g paella rice
- 400g artichoke hearts, drained and quartered
- 200g green beans, trimmed and halved
- 1 red bell pepper, thinly sliced
- 4 cloves garlic, minced
- 1 onion, finely chopped
- 2 tablespoons olive oil
- 1 teaspoon smoked paprika
- 1 teaspoon turmeric
- 1/2 teaspoon saffron threads
- 800ml vegetable broth
- 200g cherry tomatoes, halved
- 150g green olives, pitted and halved
- Fresh parsley, chopped, for garnish
- Lemon wedges, for serving

Nutrition facts per 100g:

Calories: 120
Total Fat: 4g
Saturated Fat: 0.5g
Cholesterol: 0mg
Sodium: 250mg
Total Carbohydrate: 19g
Dietary Fiber: 3g
Sugars: 2g
Protein: 3g

Preparation:

1. In a large paella pan or a wide, shallow pan, heat the olive oil over medium heat. Add the garlic and onion and sauté until fragrant and softened.
2. Add the red bell pepper and green beans to the pan, and cook for about 5 minutes until they start to soften.
3. Sprinkle in the smoked paprika, turmeric, and saffron threads. Stir well to coat the vegetables with the spices.
4. Stir in the paella rice and cook for 1-2 minutes, stirring constantly.
5. Pour in the vegetable broth and bring to a boil. Reduce the heat to low, cover the pan, and simmer for about 15 minutes until the rice is almost cooked.
6. Add the artichoke hearts, cherry tomatoes, and green olives to the pan. Stir gently to combine all the ingredients.
7. Cover the pan again and cook for an additional 5-10 minutes until the rice is fully cooked and all the flavours have melded together.
8. Remove from heat and let the paella rest, covered, for a few minutes.
9. Serve the Spanish vegan paella hot, garnished with fresh parsley and accompanied by lemon wedges for squeezing over the top.

Chapter 8: Sweet Mediterranean Treats (10 Recipes)

Greek Honey and Cinnamon Baklava

Servings: Makes approximately 24 pieces | Preparation time: 45-50 minutes

Ingredients

- 300g phyllo pastry sheets
- 200g unsalted butter, melted
- 250g walnuts, finely chopped
- 100g almonds, finely chopped
- 1 teaspoon ground cinnamon
- 1/2 teaspoon ground cloves
- 200g granulated sugar
- 200ml water
- 200ml honey
- Zest of 1 lemon
- Juice of 1/2 lemon
- Powdered sugar, for dusting

Nutrition facts per 100g:

Calories: 432 kcal
Total Fat: 25g
Saturated Fat: 8g
Trans Fat: 0g
Cholesterol: 31mg
Sodium: 110mg
Total Carbohydrate: 47g
Dietary Fiber: 2g
Sugars: 28g
Protein: 6g

Preparation:

1. Preheat the oven to 180°C and grease a rectangular baking dish with butter.
2. In a mixing bowl, combine the walnuts, almonds, ground cinnamon, ground cloves, and 50g of granulated sugar.
3. Unroll the phyllo pastry sheets and cover them with a clean, damp towel to prevent them from drying out.
4. Brush the bottom of the baking dish with melted butter and layer two sheets of phyllo pastry on top. Brush with more melted butter.
5. Sprinkle a thin layer of the nut mixture over the phyllo pastry.
6. Repeat steps 4 and 5, layering phyllo pastry, melted butter, and the nut mixture, until all the ingredients are used. Make sure to brush the top layer with melted butter as well.
7. Using a sharp knife, cut the baklava into small diamond-shaped pieces.
8. Bake in the preheated oven for about 30-35 minutes or until golden brown.
9. While the baklava bakes, prepare the syrup by combining the remaining granulated sugar, water, lemon zest, and lemon juice in a saucepan. Bring to a boil, then reduce the heat and simmer for 5 minutes. Remove from heat and stir in the honey until well combined.
10. Once the baklava is baked, remove it from the oven and pour the syrup evenly over the hot pastry.
11. Allow the baklava to cool completely in the dish, then refrigerate for a few hours or overnight for the flavours to meld together.
12. Before serving, dust the baklava with powdered sugar.

Italian Lemon Ricotta Cake

Servings: 8 | Preparation time: 50-60 minutes

Ingredients

- 250g ricotta cheese
- 200g granulated sugar
- 4 large eggs
- 150g all-purpose flour
- 1 teaspoon baking powder
- Zest of 2 lemons
- Juice of 1 lemon
- 100g unsalted butter, melted
- Icing sugar, for dusting

Nutrition facts per 100g:

Calories: 318
Total Fat: 14g
Saturated Fat: 8g
Trans Fat: 0g
Cholesterol: 98mg
Sodium: 101mg
Total Carbohydrate: 40g
Dietary Fiber: 0.5g
Sugars: 24g
Protein: 8g

Preparation:

1. Preheat the oven to 180°C (350°F). Grease and line a 20cm (8-inch) round cake tin with parchment paper.
2. In a large mixing bowl, combine the ricotta cheese, granulated sugar, and eggs. Whisk until well combined and smooth.
3. In a separate bowl, sift together the flour and baking powder. Add the lemon zest and mix well.
4. Gradually add the dry ingredients to the ricotta mixture, gently folding until just combined.
5. Stir in the lemon juice and melted butter until well incorporated.
6. Pour the batter into the prepared cake tin and smooth the top with a spatula.
7. Bake for approximately 40-45 minutes, or until a toothpick inserted into the center comes out clean.
8. Allow the cake to cool in the tin for 10 minutes, then transfer to a wire rack to cool completely.
9. Once cooled, dust the cake with icing sugar.
10. Cut into slices and serve as a delightful sweet treat.

Turkish Delight (Lokum)

Servings: Makes about 60 pieces | Preparation time: 3 hours

Ingredients

- 400g granulated sugar
- 450ml water
- 100g cornstarch
- 2 tablespoons lemon juice
- 1 tablespoon rosewater
- A few drops of pink food coloring (optional)
- 100g chopped pistachios
- 50g icing sugar, for dusting

Nutrition facts per 100g:

Calories: 334 kcal
Total Fat: 0.8g
Saturated Fat: 0.1g
Cholesterol: 0mg
Sodium: 2mg
Total Carbohydrate: 82g
Dietary Fiber: 0.4g
Sugars: 63g
Protein: 0.4g

Preparation:

1. In a large saucepan, combine the sugar and water over medium heat. Stir until the sugar completely dissolves.
2. In a separate bowl, mix the cornstarch with a little water to make a smooth paste.
3. Add the cornstarch mixture to the saucepan, stirring continuously to avoid any lumps from forming.
4. Reduce the heat to low and continue stirring steadily for about 10 minutes until the mixture thickens and becomes translucent.
5. Add the lemon juice, rosewater, and pink food coloring (if using), stirring well to combine.
6. Cook the mixture for another 5 minutes, stirring constantly.
7. Remove the saucepan from the heat and stir in the chopped pistachios.
8. Grease a square baking tray with a little oil and line it with parchment paper.
9. Pour the mixture into the prepared tray, smoothing the surface with a spatula.
10. Allow the mixture to cool completely at room temperature, then refrigerate for a few hours or overnight until set.
11. Dust a clean surface with icing sugar and carefully turn out the set Turkish Delight mixture onto it.
12. Cut the Turkish Delight into bite-sized pieces and toss them in icing sugar to prevent sticking.
13. Store the Turkish Delight in an airtight container at room temperature.

Spanish Almond Cake (Tarta de Santiago)

Servings: 8 | Preparation time: 45-50 minutes

Ingredients

- 200g ground almonds
- 200g caster sugar
- 4 large eggs
- Zest of 1 lemon
- 1 teaspoon ground cinnamon
- Icing sugar, for dusting

Nutrition facts per 100g:

Calories: 443 kcal
Total Fat: 28.6g
Saturated Fat: 2g
Cholesterol: 93mg
Sodium: 18mg
Total Carbohydrate: 34.5g
Dietary Fiber: 4g
Sugars: 29.2g
Protein: 12.5g

Preparation:

1. Preheat the oven to 180°C/160°C fan/gas mark 4. Grease and line a 23cm round cake tin.
2. In a large mixing bowl, combine the ground almonds, caster sugar, lemon zest, and cinnamon. Mix well.
3. In a separate bowl, whisk the eggs until frothy. Gradually add the whisked eggs to the almond mixture, stirring well after each addition.
4. Pour the batter into the prepared cake tin and smooth the top with a spatula.
5. Bake in the preheated oven for approximately 35-40 minutes or until the cake is golden brown and a skewer inserted into the center comes out clean.
6. Allow the cake to cool in the tin for 10 minutes, then transfer it to a wire rack to cool completely.
7. Once the cake has cooled, dust the top generously with icing sugar.
8. Serve the Spanish almond cake as a delightful Mediterranean treat with a cup of tea or coffee.

Moroccan Almond and Orange Blossom Phyllo Pastry (Mhanncha)

Servings: 8 | Preparation time: 40 minutes

Ingredients

- 200g ground almonds
- 50g caster sugar
- 1 tsp ground cinnamon
- 1/4 tsp ground ginger
- Zest of 1 orange
- 2 tbsp orange blossom water
- 200g unsalted butter, melted
- 8 sheets of filo pastry
- Icing sugar, for dusting

Nutrition facts per 100g:

Energy: 515 kcal
Protein: 10.4g
Carbohydrates: 36.7g
Sugars: 18.4g
Fat: 37.8g
Saturated fat: 16.5g
Fiber: 4.3g
Sodium: 68mg

Preparation:

1. Preheat the oven to 180°C and line a baking tray with parchment paper.
2. In a mixing bowl, combine the ground almonds, caster sugar, ground cinnamon, ground ginger, orange zest, and orange blossom water. Mix well to combine.
3. Brush a sheet of filo pastry with melted butter and place another sheet on top. Continue until you have 4 buttered sheets stacked on each other.
4. Spread half of the almond mixture evenly over the stacked filo sheets, leaving a small border at the edges.
5. Starting from one end, tightly roll the filo pastry into a log shape, enclosing the almond filling.
6. Transfer the rolled pastry onto the prepared baking tray, brushing the top with additional melted butter.
7. Repeat steps 3-6 with the remaining ingredients to make a second almond-filled pastry log.
8. Bake in the preheated oven for 25-30 minutes or until the pastry is golden brown and crisp.
9. Remove from the oven and allow to cool slightly before dusting with icing sugar.
10. To serve, cut the pastry logs into thick slices and enjoy your Moroccan almond and orange blossom phyllo pastry delights.

Greek Walnut Cake (Karidopita)

Servings: 12 | Preparation time: 45-50 minutes

Ingredients

- 250g walnuts
- 180g all-purpose flour
- 150g granulated sugar
- 3 teaspoons baking powder
- 2 teaspoons ground cinnamon
- 1/2 teaspoon ground cloves
- 1/4 teaspoon salt
- 4 large eggs
- 180ml whole milk
- 110g unsalted butter, melted
- 1 teaspoon vanilla extract
- For the syrup:
- 150g granulated sugar
- 180ml water
- 2 tablespoons lemon juice
- 1 cinnamon stick
- 1 strip of lemon zest

Nutrition facts per 100g:

Calories: 411
Total Fat: 21.5g
Saturated Fat: 5.8g
Cholesterol: 74mg
Sodium: 123mg
Total Carbohydrate: 50.4g
Dietary Fiber: 2.7g
Sugars: 34.2g
Protein: 7.5g

Preparation:

1. Preheat the oven to 180°C and grease a 20 cm square baking dish.
2. Toast the walnuts in a dry pan over medium heat for about 5 minutes until fragrant. Remove from heat, let cool, and then chop finely.
3. In a large mixing bowl, whisk together the flour, sugar, baking powder, cinnamon, cloves, and salt.
4. In a separate bowl, beat the eggs and add the milk, melted butter, and vanilla extract. Mix well.
5. Gradually pour the wet ingredients into the dry ingredients, stirring until just combined.
6. Fold in the chopped walnuts until evenly distributed.
7. Pour the batter into the prepared baking dish and smooth the top with a spatula.
8. Bake for 35-40 minutes or until a toothpick inserted into the center comes out clean.
9. While the cake is baking, prepare the syrup. In a small saucepan, combine the sugar, water, lemon juice, cinnamon stick, and lemon zest. Bring to a boil, then reduce heat and simmer for 5 minutes.
10. Remove the cake from the oven and carefully pour the hot syrup over the hot cake.
11. Allow the cake to cool completely in the baking dish before slicing and serving.

Sicilian Cannoli with Ricotta Filling

Servings: 8 cannoli | Preparation time: 45 minutes

Ingredients

For the cannoli shells:

- 200g all-purpose flour
- 20g caster sugar
- 20g unsalted butter, softened
- 1 egg yolk
- 50ml Marsala wine
- Vegetable oil, for frying

For the ricotta filling:

- 500g ricotta cheese
- 100g powdered sugar
- 1 teaspoon vanilla extract
- 50g dark chocolate, chopped
- 50g candied orange peel, finely chopped
- Icing sugar, for dusting

Nutrition facts per 100g:

Calories: 362
Total Fat: 17g
Saturated Fat: 9g
Trans Fat: 0g
Cholesterol: 56mg
Sodium: 73mg
Total Carbohydrate: 42g
Dietary Fiber: 1g
Sugars: 15g
Protein: 10g

Preparation:

1. In a large mixing bowl, combine the flour and caster sugar. Add the softened butter and mix until it resembles fine breadcrumbs. Then, add the egg yolk and Marsala wine. Mix to form a dough, then knead it gently on a floured surface until smooth. Cover the dough with a damp cloth and let it rest for 30 minutes.
2. In the meantime, prepare the ricotta filling by combining the ricotta cheese, powdered sugar, and vanilla extract in a bowl. Stir until well combined. Then, fold in the chopped dark chocolate and candied orange peel. Place the filling in the refrigerator to chill.
3. After the dough has rested, divide it into 8 equal portions. Roll each portion into a thin oval shape, around 12cm long and 8cm wide. Carefully wrap each oval-shaped dough around a cannoli tube, sealing the edges with a little water on your fingertips.
4. Heat the vegetable oil in a deep pot or fryer to 180°C. Fry the cannoli shells, 2-3 at a time, until golden brown and crispy. This should take about 3-4 minutes. Once cooked, remove them from the oil using metal tongs and place them on a paper towel-lined tray to drain excess oil. Allow them to cool slightly.
5. Once the cannoli shells have cooled, carefully slide the shells off the tubes. Fill a piping bag fitted with a wide nozzle with the prepared ricotta filling. Pipe the filling into each end of the cannoli shells, then dust both ends with icing sugar.
6. Serve the Sicilian cannoli immediately or refrigerate for later consumption.

Turkish Semolina Cake (Revani)

Servings: 8 | Preparation time: 40-45 minutes

Ingredients

- 200g semolina
- 200g caster sugar
- 4 large eggs
- 200g plain yogurt
- 100ml sunflower oil
- 1 teaspoon vanilla extract
- Zest of 1 lemon
- 1 teaspoon baking powder
- 200g ground almonds
- 250ml water
- 200g granulated sugar
- Juice of 1 lemon
- 50g flaked almonds, toasted

Nutrition facts per 100g:

Calories: 315
Total Fat: 17g
Saturated Fat: 2g
Cholesterol: 63mg
Sodium: 19mg
Total Carbohydrate: 35g
Dietary Fiber: 2g
Sugars: 21g
Protein: 7g

Preparation:

1. Preheat the oven to 180°C. Grease and line a square or rectangular baking dish with parchment paper.
2. In a large mixing bowl, whisk together the semolina, caster sugar, eggs, yogurt, sunflower oil, vanilla extract, lemon zest, baking powder, and ground almonds until well combined.
3. Pour the batter into the prepared baking dish and smooth the top with a spatula.
4. Bake in the preheated oven for 25-30 minutes or until the cake is golden brown on top and a skewer inserted into the center comes out clean.
5. While the cake is baking, prepare the syrup by combining the water, granulated sugar, and lemon juice in a saucepan. Bring to a boil, then reduce the heat and simmer for 5 minutes until the syrup slightly thickens.
6. When the cake is cooked, remove it from the oven and allow it to cool in the dish for 5 minutes. Then, using a skewer, poke holes all over the cake.
7. Slowly pour the warm syrup over the cake, allowing it to soak in.
8. Let the cake cool completely in the dish before slicing into squares or diamond shapes.
9. Serve the Turkish Semolina Cake (Revani) garnished with toasted flaked almonds for an extra crunch and enjoy!

Italian Panna Cotta with Berries

Servings: 4 | Preparation time: 25 minutes

Ingredients

- 250ml heavy cream
- 250ml milk
- 70g granulated sugar
- 1 vanilla pod, split lengthwise and seeds scraped out
- 2 gelatin sheets
- 200g mixed berries (such as strawberries, blueberries, and raspberries)
- Fresh mint leaves, for garnish

Nutrition facts per 100g:

Calories: 156
Total Fat: 8.9g
Saturated Fat: 5.5g
Cholesterol: 31mg
Sodium: 24mg
Total Carbohydrate: 16.6g
Sugars: 13.3g
Protein: 2.2g

Preparation:

1. In a saucepan, combine the heavy cream, milk, sugar, and vanilla pod with seeds. Heat the mixture over medium heat until it starts to simmer. Remove from heat and let it steep for 10 minutes.
2. Meanwhile, soak the gelatin sheets in cold water for about 5 minutes or until softened.
3. Remove the vanilla pod from the cream mixture. Squeeze out excess water from the gelatin sheets and add them to the warm cream mixture. Stir until the gelatin is completely dissolved.
4. Divide the cream mixture evenly among individual serving glasses or ramekins. Allow them to cool to room temperature, then refrigerate for at least 4 hours or until set.
5. Just before serving, wash and prepare the berries if needed. Cut larger berries into bite-sized pieces.
6. Remove the set panna cotta from the fridge. Top each portion with a generous amount of mixed berries.
7. Garnish with fresh mint leaves and serve chilled.

French Lemon Tart (Tarte au Citron) from Provence

Servings: 8 | Preparation time: 1 hour

Ingredients

For the crust:

- 200g plain flour
- 100g unsalted butter, cold and diced
- 50g icing sugar
- 1 egg yolk
- 2 tablespoons cold water

For the filling:

- 4 large eggs
- 150g granulated sugar
- 150ml freshly squeezed lemon juice (about 4 lemons)
- Zest of 2 lemons
- 150g unsalted butter, melted

For the topping:

- Icing sugar, for dusting
- Fresh mint leaves, for garnish (optional)

Nutrition facts per 100g:

Calories: 328
Fat: 19.4g
Saturated fat: 11.8g
Trans fat: 0g
Cholesterol: 137mg
Sodium: 96mg
Carbohydrates: 34.6g
Fiber: 0.8g
Sugars: 17.6g
Protein: 4.6g

Preparation:

1. In a large bowl, combine the flour and icing sugar. Add the cold butter and rub it into the flour mixture until it resembles breadcrumbs.
2. In a small bowl, whisk together the egg yolk and cold water. Pour the mixture into the flour mixture and mix until it forms a dough. Shape the dough into a ball, wrap it in cling film, and refrigerate for 30 minutes.
3. Preheat the oven to 180°C. Roll out the dough on a lightly floured surface and line a 23cm tart tin with a removable base. Press the dough into the edges of the tin and trim off any excess. Prick the base with a fork and place it back in the fridge for another 20 minutes.
4. While the crust chills, prepare the filling. In a large bowl, whisk together the eggs and sugar until well combined. Add the lemon juice, lemon zest, and melted butter, and whisk until smooth.
5. Take the crust out of the fridge and pour the lemon filling into it. Carefully transfer the tart to the preheated oven and bake for 25-30 minutes, or until the filling is set and slightly golden on top.
6. Remove the tart from the oven and allow it to cool completely. Once cooled, dust the top with icing sugar and garnish with fresh mint leaves if desired.
7. Serve chilled and enjoy this delightful French Lemon Tart!

Meal plan ideas for 7 days

Meal Plan 1

Day 1 - A Day in Greece and Italy

- *Breakfast:* Start your day with the invigorating flavours of our Honeyed Halloumi & Tomato Skewers.
- *Lunch:* For lunch, savour the richness of Greek Grilled Chicken & Hummus Wrap, a delightful mix of grilled chicken, fresh veggies, and creamy hummus wrapped in a warm pita bread.
- *Dinner:* Dinner takes you to the coasts of Italy with our Italian Baked Cod with Tomatoes and Olives - a healthy, savoury seafood dish that's easy to prepare yet loaded with flavour.
- *Snack:* Throughout the day, enjoy our Greek Tzatziki with Vegetable Crudites - a healthy, refreshing snack that's easy to enjoy anytime.
- *Dessert:* End the day with Italian Panna Cotta with Berries, a creamy, luxurious dessert that's subtly sweet and topped with fresh, tangy berries.

Day 2 - A Taste of the Mediterranean

- *Breakfast:* Awaken your senses with the Mediterranean Breakfast Salad, a fresh mix of vegetables, cheese, and crunchy nuts that's nutritious and satisfying.
- *Lunch:* Warm your soul with the Italian Minestrone Soup - a hearty, vegetable-packed soup that's both comforting and flavourful.
- *Dinner:* For dinner, enjoy Ratatouille Stuffed Zucchini Boats - a dish full of color, texture, and vibrant Mediterranean flavours.
- *Snack:* Snack on the Turkish Cheese and Spinach Gozleme - a delicious pastry filled with cheese and spinach that's perfect for a light afternoon snack.
- *Dessert:* Conclude the day with our Turkish Semolina Cake (Revani), a sweet and aromatic cake that will surely satisfy your sweet cravings.

Day 3 - Journey to Spain and Greece

- *Breakfast:* Wake up to Spanish Tortilla Bites, a hearty breakfast full of potatoes, eggs, and onions.
- *Lunch:* Come lunchtime, enjoy a refreshing Greek Salad with Lemon & Oregano Dressing, a light but filling dish that's full of classic Greek flavours.
- *Dinner:* Dinner is a Spanish affair with our Seafood Paella Valenciana, a delicious mix of rice, seafood, and vegetables cooked together for a satisfying meal.
- *Snack:* For your snack, indulge in Greek Dolmades (Stuffed Vine Leaves), a healthy and tasty snack filled with rice and herbs.
- *Dessert:* Complete your day with a Greek Honey and Cinnamon Baklava, a sweet pastry layered with nuts and sweetened with honey and cinnamon.

Day 4 - Exploring Italy and Turkey

- *Breakfast:* Your day begins with an Italian-style Bruschetta Toast, topped with fresh tomatoes, basil, and a drizzle of extra virgin olive oil.
- *Lunch:* Savour a traditional Italian Basil Pesto Pasta for lunch. The vibrant, herby pesto beautifully coats the pasta, creating a dish that's as flavourful as it is comforting.
- *Dinner:* Explore the robust flavours of Turkey with Imam Bayildi (Stuffed Eggplants). This delicious vegetarian dish is sure to leave you satisfied.
- *Snack:* Enjoy a Turkish Cucumber, Mint, and Yogurt Dip (Cacik) with some crisp vegetables or warm bread for a light, refreshing snack.
- *Dessert:* Wind down with a piece of Italian Lemon Ricotta Cake. This light, citrusy cake with a hint of sweetness is the perfect end to your day.

Day 5 - A French and Lebanese Feast

- *Breakfast:* Kickstart your day with the energy-packed Savoury Breakfast Quinoa with Olives.
- *Lunch:* Relish the French culinary classic Ratatouille with Fresh Herbs, a melody of colourful vegetables cooked with herbs.
- *Dinner:* For dinner, savour the Lebanese Lentils, Rice, and Caramelised Onions (Mujadara), a comforting, protein-rich dish full of flavour.
- *Snack:* Indulge in Lebanese Zaatar Flatbread (Manakish) for a mid-afternoon snack, a delightful flatbread topped with an aromatic blend of thyme, sesame seeds, and sumac.
- *Dessert:* Close your day with French Lemon Tart (Tarte au Citron) from Provence, a sweet and tangy dessert that will make your taste buds sing.

Day 6 - A Greek and Moroccan Adventure

- *Breakfast:* Start your day with Greek Yogurt and Honey Pancakes, light, fluffy pancakes topped with creamy Greek yogurt and a drizzle of sweet honey.
- *Lunch:* For lunch, try the Greek Lemon Rice (Avgolemono), a comforting dish combining rice, chicken broth, and a tangy lemon-egg mixture.
- *Dinner:* Dinner will take you to the heart of Morocco with a delicious Moroccan Lamb Tagine with Apricots, a slow-cooked lamb dish packed with sweet and savoury flavours.
- *Snack:* Enjoy Moroccan Spiced Carrot Hummus with some fresh veggies or warm pita bread for a healthy, flavourful snack.
- *Dessert:* Treat yourself to Greek Walnut Cake (Karidopita), a moist and syrupy dessert, for a sweet end to your day.

Day 7 - Journey to Spain and Lebanon

- *Breakfast:* Begin your day with Seville Citrus Granola, a refreshing breakfast option with the goodness of oats, nuts, and bright citrus flavours.
- *Lunch:* Enjoy Spanish Tomato Bread (Pan con Tomate) for lunch, a simple yet flavourful dish that is a staple in Spain.
- *Dinner:* Dinner is a Lebanese affair with Lebanese Chicken and Rice (Riz bi-Djaj), a flavourful dish of spiced chicken and rice.
- *Snack:* Have a Spanish Garlic Shrimp (Gambas al Ajillo) for your snack, a savoury and garlicky dish perfect for a light bite.
- *Dessert:* End your culinary journey with a delightful Spanish Almond Cake (Tarta de Santiago), a rich and nutty dessert that will leave you wanting more.
- lge in Greek Dolmades (Stuffed Vine Leaves), a healthy and tasty snack filled with rice and herbs.
- *Dessert:* Complete your day with a Greek Honey and Cinnamon Baklava, a sweet pastry layered with nuts and sweetened with honey and cinnamon.

Meal Plan 2

Day 1 - Turkish Delights

- *Breakfast:* Start your day with Honeyed Halloumi & Tomato Skewers, a perfect balance of sweet, salty, and tangy flavours.
- *Lunch:* Turkish Lentil Soup (Mercimek Çorbası) will make a comforting and hearty lunch.
- *Dinner:* For dinner, let's stay with the Turkish theme and have Imam Bayildi (Stuffed Eggplants), a delicious and satisfying vegetarian dish.
- *Snack:* Try Turkish Cheese and Spinach Gozleme for a savoury snack.
- *Dessert:* Enjoy a piece of Turkish Delight (Lokum) for a sweet ending to your day.

Day 2 - Italian Treasures

- *Breakfast:* Wake up to the Italian-style Bruschetta Toast topped with fresh tomatoes and basil.
- *Lunch:* For lunch, the classic Italian Minestrone Soup will be nourishing and tasty.
- *Dinner:* Enjoy Italian Baked Cod with Tomatoes and Olives, a simple yet flavourful seafood dish.
- *Snack:* Have Italian Marinated Olives with Citrus and Fennel for an afternoon bite.
- *Dessert:* Close your day with a slice of Italian Lemon Ricotta Cake, a sweet and zesty treat.

Day 3 - Greek Adventures

- *Breakfast:* Start with Greek-Style Yoghurt Parfait, a delicious and nutritious layered breakfast.
- *Lunch:* Savour Greek Salad with Lemon & Oregano Dressing for a refreshing and filling lunch.
- *Dinner:* Dinner is Greek Style Baked Chicken Souvlaki, full of classic Greek flavours.
- *Snack:* Greek Spinach and Feta Cheese Triangles (Spanakopita) make a delicious snack.
- *Dessert:* End your day with Greek Honey and Cinnamon Baklava, a sweet pastry layered with nuts and honey.

Day 4 - Moroccan Magic

- *Breakfast:* Begin with Olive and Feta Scramble, a hearty and flavourful start to your day.
- *Lunch:* Moroccan Chickpea and Vegetable Stew for lunch will offer an exotic flavour punch.
- *Dinner:* Have Moroccan Lamb Tagine with Apricots for dinner, a slow-cooked, flavourful Moroccan classic.
- *Snack:* Try Moroccan Zaalouk (Aubergine and Tomato Dip) with some warm bread.
- *Dessert:* Enjoy a slice of Moroccan Almond and Orange Blossom Phyllo Pastry (M'hanncha) to end your day on a sweet note.

Day 5 - Spanish Fiesta

- *Breakfast:* Start your day with Spanish Tortilla Bites, a flavourful and filling breakfast.
- *Lunch:* Spanish Tomato Bread (Pan con Tomate) makes a simple, yet delicious lunch.
- *Dinner:* For dinner, Seafood Paella Valenciana will bring the flavours of Spain to your table.
- *Snack:* Have some Spanish Patatas Bravas for a satisfying snack.
- *Dessert:* Spanish Almond Cake (Tarta de Santiago) is the perfect sweet ending to your day.

Day 6 - Lebanese Love

- *Breakfast:* Begin your day with a Mediterranean Breakfast Salad, a fresh and healthy start to your day.
- *Lunch:* Try the Lebanese Falafel Wrap, a flavourful and hearty lunch option.
- *Dinner:* For dinner, Lebanese Lentils, Rice and Caramelised Onions (Mujadara) will make a delicious and filling meal.
- *Snack:* Enjoy Lebanese Zaatar Flatbread (Manakish) as an evening snack.
- *Dessert:* Indulge in a sweet, creamy Lebanese Milk Pudding (Mahalabia) to end your day.

Day 7 - French Flavours

- *Breakfast:* Start your day with Tomato and Basil Savoury Oatmeal, a hearty and nutritious breakfast.
- *Lunch:* For lunch, the Warm French Lentil Salad with Dijon Vinaigrette is both flavourful and satisfying.
- *Dinner:* For dinner, enjoy the Provençal Ratatouille with Fresh Herbs, a colourful medley of vegetables cooked to perfection.
- *Snack:* Have some Olive Tapenade Crostini for a light and flavourful snack.
- *Dessert:* Finish your week-long Mediterranean culinary adventure with the classic French dessert - Lemon Tart (Tarte au Citron) from Provence. Enjoy this sweet and tangy treat as the perfect end to your week.

Final Bites

Closing Thoughts on the Mediterranean Diet

The Mediterranean Diet has long been hailed as one of the healthiest and most sustainable ways of eating. With its focus on whole foods, fresh produce, and simple but flavourful ingredients, it is no wonder that people from the Mediterranean region have been enjoying these super-amazing dishes for centuries. Throughout this book, we have explored the rich flavours and diverse culinary traditions of the Mediterranean. From Greek salads and Spanish tapas to Italian pasta and Moroccan tagines, the recipes presented here offer a taste of the Mediterranean's vibrant and delicious cuisine.

But the Mediterranean Diet is not solely about the food itself. It is a way of life, a philosophy that embraces balance, mindfulness, and the joy of eating. It is a reminder that food is meant to be savoured, that meals are meant to be shared with loved ones, and that nourishing the body is an act of self-care. At its core, the Mediterranean Diet is about simplicity. It encourages us to cook with seasonal ingredients, to make use of what's available locally, and to embrace the abundance of fresh vegetables, fruits, whole grains, and lean proteins that nature provides. By doing so, we not only support our own health but also the health of the planet.

One of the key components of the Mediterranean Diet is the use of olive oil as the primary source of fat. Olive oil, with its heart-healthy monounsaturated fats and wealth of antioxidants, is a staple in Mediterranean cooking. It adds depth and richness to dishes while providing numerous health benefits. Whether drizzled over a salad, used for sautéing vegetables, or incorporated into a homemade vinaigrette, olive oil serves as the liquid gold that ties Mediterranean cuisine together. In addition to olive oil, herbs and spices play a prominent role in Mediterranean cooking. From the aromatic basil in pesto to the earthy cumin in Moroccan stews, these flavourful additions not only enhance the taste of dishes but also offer a myriad of health benefits. It's truly amazing how a pinch of herbs or a sprinkle of spices can transform a simple meal into a culinary masterpiece.

Another defining characteristic of the Mediterranean Diet is the abundance of plant-based foods. With an emphasis on vegetables, fruits, legumes, and whole grains, this way of eating provides a wealth of essential nutrients, fiber, and antioxidants. It promotes good heart health, reduces the risk of chronic diseases, and supports overall well-being. By filling our plates with colourful, plant-based foods, we nourish our bodies and promote a sustainable future. But the Mediterranean Diet isn't just about what we eat; it's also about how we eat. The Mediterranean lifestyle encourages us to slow down, take pleasure in our meals, and practice mindful eating. By savouring each bite, chewing slowly, and tuning in to our body's hunger and fullness cues, we can better appreciate the flavours and textures of our food while also developing a healthier relationship with eating.

As we come to the end of this culinary journey through the Mediterranean, let us remember that the Mediterranean Diet is more than just a collection of recipes. It is a celebration of life, a way to honor our bodies, and a reminder of the rich cultural heritage that comes with each dish. So, let us embrace this lifestyle, experiment with new ingredients and flavours, and make the Mediterranean Diet a part of our everyday enjoyment. In closing, I hope that this book has inspired you to embark on your own Mediterranean adventure, to explore the vibrant flavours and wholesome ingredients that this way of eating has to offer. May your kitchen be filled with the delicious aromas and the joyful spirit of the Mediterranean, and may your meals be a source of nourishment, satisfaction, and pure culinary delight.

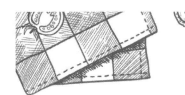

EXCLUSIVE BONUS

40 Weight Loss Recipes

&

14 Days Meal Plan

Scan the QR-Code and receive
the FREE download:

Disclaimer

This book contains the opinions and ideas of the author and is meant to teach the reader informative and helpful knowledge while due care should be taken by the user in the application of the information provided. The instructions and strategies are possibly not right for every reader and there is no guarantee that they work for everyone. Using this book and implementing the information/recipes therein contained is explicitly your own responsibility and risk. This work with all its contents does not guarantee the correctness, completion, quality, or correctness of the provided information. Misinformation or misprints cannot be completely eliminated.

Printed in Great Britain
by Amazon

26813417R00094